"Biblical counseling, grounded in the sufficiency and authority of Scripture, is essential to the health of the church. Here is a remarkably helpful introduction to pastoral counseling, brimming with sage, biblical wisdom for both new and seasoned pastors. Every pastor needs this book."

R. Albert Mohler Jr., President and Joseph Emerson Brown Professor of Christian Theology, The Southern Baptist Theological Seminary

"This book is faithful to God, thoughtful, and realistic about people. It's clearly written, simple, and practical. We all struggle. How can you and your church learn to care well? Take this book to heart."

David Powlison, Executive Director, Christian Counseling and Educational Foundation

"This is a book on how pastors should listen to their church members and speak to them, a book on how we should love. It is eminently biblical, practical, and refreshing. Perhaps we should make it required reading for all new elders."

Mark Dever, Senior Pastor, Capitol Hill Baptist Church, Washington, DC; President, 9Marks

"This book demonstrates to busy pastors that the work of counseling is not only required but possible. If you are overwhelmed by this critical task, Pierre and Reju will steer you through the confusion. Their deep convictions about Scripture have been tested in the crucible of pastoral ministry. I am excited for you to learn from them in these pages."

Heath Lambert, Executive Director, Association of Certified Biblical Counselors; Associate Professor of Biblical Counseling, The Southern Baptist Theological Seminary

"*The best primer* for pastoral counseling I've read—and I've read many. Frankly, it is the equivalent of at least two excellent seminary courses on pastoral counseling. Read it, apply it, and be equipped for the personal ministry of God's Word."

Robert W. Kellemen, Vice President, Institutional Development; Chair, Biblical Counseling Department, Crossroads Bible College

"A gem on the privilege and necessity of shepherding God's people, this winsomely written primer is loaded with invaluable perspectives, guidelines, and insights on how to love others well during their time of need. I wholeheartedly commend it."

Robert K. Cheong, Pastor of Care, Sojourn Community Church, Louisville, Kentucky

"A balanced approach to both theory and methodology in one volume, this book will be a great asset for the busy pastor who wants to do biblical counseling but doesn't know where to start. One's appetite for truth and practical help will be satisfied, and the fear of counselees and their problems will lessen."

Rod Mays, Adjunct Professor of Counseling, Reformed Theological Seminary; Executive Pastor, Mitchell Road Presbyterian Church, Greenville, South Carolina

"One of the most important and perhaps most overwhelming things ministers do is counseling. This book provides pastors with a basic framework to approach the troubles and suffering of the people they are privileged to shepherd."

Justin S. Holcomb, Episcopal Priest; Professor of Christian Thought, Gordon-Conwell Theological Seminary

"Pastoring is hard work, a labor of love that requires theological know-how and the heart of Jesus for people who are suffering or straying. This is the best primer available, pointing pastors to the wisdom found only in the Bible and outlining basic methods and procedures for personal ministry."

Sam R. Williams, Professor of Counseling, Southeastern Baptist Theological Seminary

"Pierre and Reju faithfully point pastors to the life-transforming good news of Jesus Christ as both the means and the goal of change in counseling. I wish I had read such a book when I began ministry. It would have alleviated many fears about counseling and better equipped me to shepherd my congregation. This primer will be at the top of the list for our interns to read for pastoral counseling."

Phil A. Newton, Senior Pastor, South Woods Baptist Church, Memphis, Tennessee

"Anything we don't understand is scarier than it needs to be. This book does an excellent job overviewing the counseling process, identifying common pitfalls, and providing intuitive protocols. It will orient you to your role in the process so that your fears do not distract you from caring for God's people."

Brad Hambrick, Pastor of Counseling, The Summit Church, Durham, North Carolina

"A counseling book where the starting point is the Word of God and the objective is a deeper understanding of the gospel, this book is loaded with practical, scriptural insights that can be applied immediately. You'll find yourself referring to it constantly when counseling."

Robby Gallaty, Senior Pastor, Brainerd Baptist Church, Chattanooga, Tennessee

"Pierre and Reju have given pastors everywhere a much-needed primer on biblical counseling. This book will tear down the walls of anxiety that pastors feel as they counsel their congregants in a manner worthy of the gospel."

Dave Furman, Senior Pastor, Redeemer Church of Dubai

"Here is a great help for busy pastors who seek to fulfill their shepherding role through counseling hurting people. The step-by-step approach discusses a variety of issues counselors face and offers practical advice for each stage in the context of developing a culture of discipleship within the church."

Richard P. Belcher Jr., Professor of Old Testament and Academic Dean, Reformed Theological Seminary, Charlotte, North Carolina

"A complex subject like pastoral counseling is well served by a helpful, biblical, and condensed guide like *The Pastor and Counseling*. Pierre and Reju deftly summarize the most important aspects of soul care. I highly recommend this book to any pastor as a starter or refresher."

Stuart W. Scott, Associate Professor of Biblical Counseling, The Southern Baptist Theological Seminary

"What more could the pastor ask for than a manual providing reasonable, understandable helps on shepherding the flock. Giving hope and help to shepherds in their God-given calling, this book is a must read."

Thomas Zempel, Pastor of Care Ministry, Colonial Baptist Church, Cary, North Carolina; Professor of Counseling, Shepherds Seminary

"This is one of the first books every shepherd of a local flock should own. It is at once reverently Christ-centered and accessibly practical. Step-by-step the authors outline how pastors can walk alongside hurting people, giving hope and help."

Chris Brauns, Pastor, The Red Brick Church, Stillman Valley, Illinois

THE

[# PASTOR]

AND

[# COUNSELING]

THE BASICS of SHEPHERDING

MEMBERS in NEED

JEREMY PIERRE & DEEPAK REJU

:: CROSSWAY®

WHEATON, ILLINOIS

The Pastor and Counseling: The Basics of Shepherding Members in Need

Copyright © 2015 by Jeremy Pierre and Deepak Reju

Published by Crossway
        1300 Crescent Street
        Wheaton, Illinois 60187

Chapter 7 is taken in part from: Deepak Reju and Mark Dever, "The Health of the Church and Biblical Counseling," in *Christ-Centered Biblical Counseling*, ed. James MacDonald. Copyright © 2013 by Biblical Counseling Coalition. Published by Harvest House Publishers, Eugene, Oregon 97402. www.harvesthousepublishers.com. Used by permission.

Cover design: Studio Gearbox

Cover image: © Veer

First printing 2015

Printed in the United States of America

Trade paperback ISBN: 978-1-4335-4512-2
ePub ISBN: 978-1-4335-4515-3
PDF ISBN: 978-1-4335-4513-9
Mobipocket ISBN: 978-1-4335-4514-6

Library of Congress Cataloging-in-Publication Data
Pierre, Jeremy, 1979– author.
  The pastor and counseling : the basics of shepherding
members in need / Jeremy Pierre and Deepak Reju.
     pages cm.— (9Marks)
  Includes bibliographical references and index.
  1. Pastoral counseling. I. Reju, Deepak, 1969– author.
II. Title.
BV4012.2.P48   2015
253.5—dc23   2014028659

Crossway is a publishing ministry of Good News Publishers.

VP		30	29	28	27	26	25	24	23	22	21	20
19	18	17	16	15	14	13	12	11	10	9	8	7

To pastors
who bear many troubles
not theirs

To honor the One
who took a world of trouble
not his

Contents

Series Preface

The 9Marks series of books is premised on two basic ideas. First, the local church is far more important to the Christian life than many Christians today perhaps realize. We at 9Marks believe that a healthy Christian is a healthy church member.

Second, local churches grow in life and vitality as they organize their lives around God's Word. God speaks. Churches should listen and follow. It's that simple. When a church listens and follows, it begins to look like the One it is following. It reflects his love and holiness. It displays his glory. A church will look like him as it listens to him. By this token, the reader might notice that all "9 marks," taken from Mark Dever's book *Nine Marks of a Healthy Church*, 3rd ed. (Wheaton, IL: Crossway, 2013), begin with the Bible:

- expositional preaching
- biblical theology
- a biblical understanding of the gospel
- a biblical understanding of conversion
- a biblical understanding of evangelism
- a biblical understanding of church membership
- a biblical understanding of church discipline
- a biblical understanding of discipleship and growth
- a biblical understanding of church leadership

More can be said about what churches should do in order to be healthy, such as pray. But these nine practices are the ones that we believe are most often overlooked today (unlike prayer). So our basic message to churches is, don't look to the best business practices or the latest styles; look to God. Start by listening to God's Word again.

Out of this overall project comes the 9Marks series of books. These volumes intend to examine the nine marks more closely and from different angles. Some target pastors. Some target church members. Hopefully all will combine careful biblical examination, theological reflection, cultural consideration, corporate application, and even a bit of individual exhortation. The best Christian books are always both theological and practical.

It's our prayer that God will use this volume and the others to help prepare his bride, the church, with radiance and splendor for the day of his coming.

The Pastor and Wednesday Morning

It's Tuesday afternoon, and you are waging war with your inbox when your secretary buzzes. A church member is asking to speak to you, and it's trouble. With a quick prayer that is more like a sigh, you pick up the phone and wade into a half-hour conversation that confuses you and, you're sure, confuses her too. You hang up, your mind racing with what to do with this sudden revelation of just how bad things are between her and her husband. You'll be seeing the two of them first thing the next day to iron some of this out. How do you begin to prepare for Wednesday morning?

Pastors and lay leaders alike are familiar with phone calls like this. Probably too familiar. Stubborn depression, heart-wrenching adultery, volcanic anger, chronic miscommunica-tion, guilt-ridden pornography struggles, calorie-phobic eating disorders, recurrent cancer, hidden same-sex attraction, suicidal thinking—and that's the short list. Life in a fallen world is touched with misery. For some, it's submerged in it. That goes for folks inside the church as well as those outside.

This is why you are a pastor. God has called you to shepherd his sheep, and often those sheep are hurting, confused, or stubborn. But it's not always clear how to care for them, especially in the more complex situations that weigh them down. You may or may not think of yourself as a counseling pastor, but the bottom line is that you are called to labor for your people in these unsettling problems. And this is a worthy labor.

We offer this primer because in our line of work we frequently get last-minute phone calls from pastors who need help thinking carefully through tough situations at church.

> In fifteen minutes, I am meeting with a couple who are about to get a divorce. Here's what I'm thinking of doing . . .

> A young man at our church just admitted to me that he has same-sex attraction. I need to follow up, but I don't know what to say . . .

> Some parents at my church recently put it together that their daughter is anorexic. Is there a place to refer them to?

Most pastors are short on time and burdened with many other responsibilities. Add to this a few common facts that plague the work of a pastor:

- Most seminary students take just one or two counseling classes in their degree programs. They often underestimate how much counseling they will do when they reach their first pastorate.
- Most pastors enter the pastorate to preach and teach, not to counsel. They counsel because it is an expected part of the job, not because they are excited to do it.

- Both smaller and larger churches have people who have made messes of their lives. Small churches, especially those in rural areas, often have very few resources in their community to draw on for help. A pastor and church are sometimes the only available resources.
- Church members expect their pastor to help them with their struggles. After all, the members fund the pastor's salary. They expect him to give them his time, often a lot of it. They may even assume the pastor has instant access to the Bible's answer for the troubles of life.
- Weak sheep tend to consume a disproportionate amount of the pastor's schedule with their problems, demands, and sometimes just general selfishness. Often this comes with very little gratitude to God for the Christlike care given through their pastor and the church.
- Most church members let their problems get far worse than they need to before they overcome pride and come in for help. Thoughts like "I don't want the pastor to think poorly of me" or "I can handle this on my own" deceive them. If they had sought help earlier, it would have saved everyone a whole lot of sweat and tears.

What should a pastor do with all this? He may have very little training in counseling. He may have weak sheep making exorbitant demands on his time. He may have precious little relational help to draw on in an unhealthy church. It doesn't sound all that promising, does it?

DEAR PASTOR, CAN WE HELP YOU?

We want to help by giving you a basic framework to approach your people's troubles. You may not have a lot of time. You may be fearful of messing someone up permanently. You may simply not want to deal with this stuff. So what you need is both a reminder that the gospel of Jesus Christ is powerful in these situations and some practical guidance for ministering in light of that power.

Here's what we would like to cover in this short book. In part 1, made up of the first three chapters, we cover the *concept* of counseling. In chapter 1, we set out a vision for what it means to labor for your people. Our point is simple: shepherds shepherd. Pastors are about the task of making disciples, and discipleship will often include counseling people through difficult situations. This fact should neither annoy nor overwhelm you. It doesn't necessarily need to thrill you either, but it should make you see caring for troubled people as part of the privilege of loving Jesus. Feed his sheep. In chapter 2, we help you know how to prepare for counseling—how it starts, who starts it, and how to arrange things to run as smoothly as possible. Chapter 3 lays out the basic method of counseling. We explain a helpful technique to explore a person's trouble and have something redemptive to say to him or her. We discuss the types of questions to ask, the pertinent areas of a person's life to explore, and how to respond in biblically helpful ways.

The second part, chapters 4–6, traces out the *process* of counseling, from the initial meeting to the final conversation. We give tips for recognizing heart dynamics, understanding problems theologically, and employing redemptive strategies for change. We want these chapters to help you answer the question, what does the process of caring for this person look like?

The third and final part, chapters 7 and 8, explains the *context* of counseling. Pastoral counseling occurs within both the church community and a community of resources outside the church. Chapter 7 deals with the reality that you, the pastor, cannot labor alone. It's not possible for you to do everything and still stay sane yourself. So we'll help you think about what it means to develop a culture of discipleship in your church that will supplement and enrich whatever counseling occurs. What does it mean to develop a culture in which members help one another thrive in their faith? Chapter 8 then looks outside to the community to see what counselors, doctors, or other relational resources are available. Is it ever wise to refer outside the church? If you do, how can you be confident a particular doctor is going to help and not hurt your church member? What if you can't find a like-minded counselor in your community, but only those who work from a naturalistic standpoint? Questions abound.

We close the book with a number of helpful practical resources, from a simple definition of biblical counseling to a method for taking notes. These are meant for your use, and we hope they aid you in this worthy labor.

THE REAL POWER IN COUNSELING— JESUS CHRIST

Honestly, no one expects one little book to change your world. Our goal is not to enable you to handle anything that comes your way. The goal, rather, is to give you confidence that in the gospel you have the categories you need to navigate the troubles of your people. Your confidence is not in some super-developed counseling technique, or even in yourself, but in God's power to change people.

Real confidence is rooted in the life-transforming power of the good news of Jesus Christ. After all, Jesus is the model of how human beings function best. And he came to a malfunctioning world as a substitute for malfunctioning human beings like us. Sin estranges us from God. It estranges everything from God. This is why we suffer and this is why we sin. But Jesus reconciles what was estranged by making payment for sin by his death. And now Jesus lives again, transforming people to live according to his righteousness, according to a reestablished relationship with God. It is God, through his glorious Son, who changes people.

Here's what we mean more specifically: We human beings were created to display God's character in the way we think, in what we desire, and in how we act. When a hardened thought, a lustful desire, or a selfish intention emerges in the human heart, that heart is failing to display the character of its Creator, which is patient, pure, and generous to others. In short, everything inside and outside a person was designed to glorify God.

Jesus's heart was the only one that perfectly displayed the character of God—because he is God himself. But he is also human, like us. Therefore, he is fit to be our representative, our example, our rescuer (Heb. 4:14–16). For counseling, we should therefore keep the following in mind:

- Jesus Christ is *the means of change*. Believing his gospel changes our hearts' responses. All theoretical wisdom and practical advice in counseling should most centrally promote a relationship with Jesus Christ through faith.
- Jesus Christ is *the goal of change*. Displaying his character is the model of maturity we strive for. Circumstances may not change and problems may not go away through counseling, but God promises the power to respond in ways that reflect the trusting obedience of his Son.

Counseling in its simplest form is one person seeking to walk alongside another person who has lost his or her way. Professional training or academic programs can be very helpful for honing skill, but even if you have not had these, you can counsel if you wholeheartedly embrace God's Word as that which shows people their greatest needs and their greatest hope.

This labor is worthy of your time, pastor. Our hope is to equip you with the basic tools to start. The framework we lay out here is our attempt to be bold with gospel truth toward the problems that unsettle our people. Frankly, it would be much easier to sweep them all away with generalized pulpit instruction or refer people off somewhere. But it's a worthy labor for a pastor to care skillfully for his people.

Part One

CONCEPT

ONE

Laboring for Your People

Shepherds do not smell good. At least, good shepherds do not smell good. A good shepherd identifies with stinking sheep, and the scent rubs off.

But shepherds stink not only because they smell like sheep. They stink because they smell like sweat. And blood, too. Like common laborers, their faces are streaked and their backs are bent. Like common soldiers, their eyes are strained and their arms are scarred. Like both, they often feel overspent and undersupplied. And they've made peace with the fact that this kind of work requires as much. You'll never meet a good shepherd who is still shower-fresh by the afternoon.

In the same way, you'll never meet a good pastor who has a breezy attitude toward his task. He does not bemoan the hard work required to care for the stubborn and the hurting while still feeding and protecting everyone else. Sure, every pastor has days when he is tempted to look heavenward and ask, why the constant problems from these people? But he finds the faith to accept that his task is hard. God made it that way to empty a pastor of himself, so that he may be filled with the power of Christ.

PUBLIC MINISTRY, PERSONAL PROBLEMS

We have never heard the explicit claim that ministry is easy. But we have seen many pastors try to arrange it to be. We've also seen plenty of men head into the pastorate for a pulpit ministry. What they mean by *pulpit ministry* is getting paid to preach and teach, with perhaps a pastoral visit here and there. They know personal ministry and counseling are important, so they usually plan to grow the church budget through their amazing pulpit skills, then hire an associate pastor to do everything else.

We do not mean to sound caustic. We were once young men with visions of leading a loyal people into the great unknown through eloquent exposition and piercing application, the power of the Word radiating from the pulpit like blazing light in the dusky culture. Husbands would take the hands of their wives during our sermons and repent in bitter tears that afternoon. Addicts would decide then and there to never indulge again. Depressed people would come out of their fog under the sound of our voices. Our preaching ministry would be strong enough to make the counseling ministry unnecessary. Or at least mostly unnecessary. Sure, there would be a straggling nut-job here and there, but the church would be healthy because of the preaching ministry.

But two things kept us from persisting in this dream: experience and the Bible. Experience is a strict schoolmaster. It points out right away that we start out as pretty crummy preachers. Even as we become less crummy, we will find that improved preaching does not necessarily correlate with less trouble in the lives of our people. In fact, pick your favorite preacher, and you will see a church with a bigger budget but no less trouble in the life of its people. Experience won't permit the illusion that preaching is all there is to ministry.

Just to be crystal clear, preaching is *the* vital and central ministry of the Word in the mission of the church. It is a primary purpose of the body's gathering and is foundational to any personal ministry we do. So do not misunderstand our intention here. We are not calling into question the primacy of the preaching ministry. We are merely pointing out that it is not the only place that the ministry of the Word happens in the life of the church.

Experience alone would not be a sufficient teacher to establish this point. Better than simply learning from what doesn't work in the real world is learning what constitutes shepherding by looking to the Bible.

PERSONAL MINISTRY IN SCRIPTURE

Peter's eyes were probably weary as the morning sun was just starting to warm the beach. He probably studied Jesus's resurrected face closely as they ate breakfast in silence, all the disciples too timid to ask if it was really he. They were waiting for Jesus to start the conversation.

"Simon, son of John, do you love me more than these?"

You know the story. Three times Jesus asked Peter if he truly loved him. By the third time, Peter was grieved that Jesus would seem so unconvinced by his affirmative answers. But each time, Jesus was instructing Peter how to demonstrate genuine love for him: "Feed my sheep" (John 21:15–19). Loving Jesus involves caring for those who are his. And caring for those who are his will involve death. For Peter, it was literal death. Jesus predicted "by what kind of death he was to glorify God" (v. 19).

Ministry Is Suffering

While we recognize that Peter's calling as an apostle was unique to him, we also understand that the path of following Jesus in leading his church will include both labor in feeding sheep and suffering at the hands of others.

Many years later, the seasoned Peter would make this connection urgently clear:

> So I exhort the elders among you, as a fellow elder and a witness of the sufferings of Christ, as well as a partaker in the glory that is going to be revealed: shepherd the flock of God that is among you, exercising oversight, not under compulsion, but willingly, as God would have you; not for shameful gain, but eagerly; not domineering over those in your charge, but being examples to the flock. And when the chief Shepherd appears, you will receive the unfading crown of glory. (1 Pet. 5:1–4)

Peter's authority as an apostle was due, in part, to his witness of the sufferings of Christ. He focused on Christ's suffering because it was necessary to the glory to be revealed. This is a major theme of Peter's letter (1 Pet. 1:6–7, 11; 2:21–25; 3:13–17, 18–22; 4:1, 7, 12–19). Peter would one day participate in this glory, and so will every pastor who shepherds the flock of God until Christ's return.

But to get there, shepherds will suffer. Why else would Peter have to instruct his readers to take on this task willingly, even eagerly, and not under obligation? We don't naturally take on tasks that do not profit us ("not for shameful gain") or that we cannot ensure will go our way ("not domineering over those in your charge"). We don't naturally want to get close enough to model faithfulness in suffering. But the words of Jesus to Peter that morning on the beach probably echoed in the apostle's mind as he penned this exhortation to his fellow pastors. "Shepherd the flock of God" sounds a lot like "Feed my lambs."

Peter saw Jesus ascend into heaven, and it made whatever toil he had to face on behalf of his people well worth it. He knew that Jesus took his place in heaven to be the chief Shepherd, one who would be ultimately responsible for watching over every sheep. This is indeed a worthy labor.

Ministry Is Personal

But so far, we have only shown that Scripture indicates shepherding God's flock to involve labor and suffering; we have not yet shown that the toil is not merely in public proclamation, but also in personal ministry. To do so, let's look to Paul as a prime example of a man who toiled in public proclamation while also engaging in the labor of personal ministry.

Paul was a public beacon of gospel preaching, and he was called by God to suffer in this labor (Acts 9:15–16). He proclaimed the gospel openly in the synagogues, and this brought threats of death (9:20–25). Paul proclaimed the good news publicly in Cyprus (13:4), Antioch (13:14), Iconium (14:1), various cities of Lycaonia (14:6–7), and countless other places. A major portion of Paul's ministry was the public proclamation of the gospel.

But if we were to conclude there, we would have to ignore significant portions of Paul's ministry. His letters to the churches displayed the heart of a man who had labored many long hours in caring for God's people. In fact, he refers to his suffering and labor amid people as the credentials that prove his calling by God in opposition to those who used earthly impressiveness to prove theirs. He underwent beatings, stonings, and shipwreck to labor personally for God's people (2 Cor. 11:23–30). Paul speaks of his own ministry as flowing from "affectionate desire" for those under his care, a desire so strong that he, Silvanus, and Timothy "were ready to share with you not only the gospel of God but also our own selves, because you had become very dear to us" (1 Thess. 2:8). He underwent "labor and toil," earning a living so as not to be a burden on them, so that he could say, "Like a father with his children, we exhorted each one of you and encouraged you and charged you to walk in a manner worthy of God, who calls you into his own kingdom and glory" (2:11–12). There's a man who labored among his people for their good.

Paul's was not a pulpit-only ministry. His care for others didn't end with their participation in his public ministry, which is a temptation for all pastors. Pastors, if we are viewing our job primarily in terms of our public influence, then we will lose the heart for personal ministry. Sometimes we are more bothered by the thought of people leaving our church than we are by the thought of them hurting. But this was not Paul's heart, and it wasn't the heart of the One he followed.

The rest of the New Testament expounds on the personal nature of pastoral ministry. Three of its teachings will prove helpful in our consideration of the task of counseling. Personal ministry involves (1) identifying with the weakness and sin of people, (2) speaking to God on behalf of people, and (3) speaking to people on behalf of God.

Pastoral labor involves identifying with the weakness and sin of people. Condescension. We usually use this word negatively because it implies that a person thinks he is superior to others, yet resigns himself to coming down to their level. But the term *condescension* is perfectly appropriate to Jesus's association with sinners, since he *does* exist on a plane above ours. He existed in perfect joy and satisfaction with the Father, God of all, bright and majestic, served by the flaming angels of heaven, with no obligation to people below, wicked and sorrowful from sin. Yet the only being in all the universe who should be served by everyone instead served everyone. He considered the interests of others (Phil. 2:4) by not insisting on staying in the contented glory of heaven that was his divine possession (2:6). Instead, he served us by identifying with our troubles (2:7), particularly our main trouble: death (2:8). Death is a problem we could never have solved. We needed the help of another. And the One who helped tells us to follow his example: "Have this mind among yourselves, which is yours in Christ Jesus" (2:5).

Death to ourselves for the good of others requires getting involved in their troubles. Jesus put himself in the position necessary to sympathize with weak people: "For we do not have a high priest who is unable to sympathize with our weaknesses, but one who in every respect has been tempted as we are, yet without sin" (Heb. 4:15). Jesus can sympathize with us because he exposed himself to the actual experience of temptation (v. 15b). He entered as a participant in the danger of a sin-cursed world and now can deal gently with the weak and wayward since he understands their weakness (5:2). He who could rightfully exist for all eternity without ever experiencing pain or distress entered a reality where he was characterized by both. He was a "man of sorrows, and acquainted with grief" (Isa. 53:3).

And so it is with pastors serving Jesus's flock. Jesus stands in the muddy waters of his people's weakness, waywardness, and suffering, and he beckons the pastor to come join him there. Pastors who want to follow have to trudge into unknown waters. The grimy surface keeps them from knowing how deep it gets, and the odor warns them of something unpleasant beneath the surface. But they trust the One who's calling them into it.

Pastor, you are freed to imitate this pattern for the good of your people. Every pastor is a servant of Jesus, and a servant is not greater than his master (John 13:16). You are called to take on the risk and the toil of people's problems. Like Jesus, you help people who, in a sense, have no business demanding help from you. If the chief Shepherd is dirty and cut up, so too those who follow him in this task. This does not necessarily mean that you become the primary counselor of your church, but it certainly means that you need to learn the skills necessary for serving your people in their trouble.

Pastoral labor involves speaking to God on behalf of people. Pastors ought to be eager and constant in prayer. There are at least two advantages to prayer that flow from close association with people in their troubles.

First, personally caring for your people will make your prayers more fervent. A pastor who labors lightly among his people often labors lightly before God. A pastor who agonizes with people will feel some agony in his prayers on their behalf. When pastors move away from personal ministry to almost exclusively public or administrative tasks, they can easily lose sight of the profound needs in their midst, and this will have a numbing effect on their prayers. Jesus taught us to pray to the Father with kingdom desperation (Matt. 6:7–13), and bearing the burdens of your people will drive you to desperate prayer.

When a pastor witnesses the miserable effects of anger in a home, sits with a discouraged widow who feels like she should be over her grief after two years, comes alongside a teenager who's convinced he's the worst pervert in the world, talks with a man who's had it with his marriage—suddenly his desperate need for wisdom becomes more apparent. Witnessing the desperation that sin and its effects cause in people's lives will bring a holy desperation to a pastor's prayers. The misery of the world is often what prompts the prayers of God's people. And pastors must not insulate themselves from this prompting.

Second, personally caring for your people will make your prayers more dependent. Nothing feels more futile than talking a depressed person out of despondency or an anorexic girl out of her unrealistic self-assessment. One of the best ways to feel your inability to change anything is giving counsel to abuse victims or perpetrators, to people with stubborn attitudes or foggy minds, to those who despise you and the Bible you're opening. Coming alongside people in impossible circumstances will be a constant reminder to the pastor of his need for the God of the impossible.

Pastoral labor involves speaking to people on behalf of God. Pastoral labor—including personal ministry—is also closely associated with proclamation. It is outright toil to proclaim Christ to people. Once again, Paul is our pastoral example: "Him we proclaim, warning everyone and teaching everyone with all wisdom, that we may present everyone mature in Christ. For this I toil, struggling with all his energy that he powerfully works within me" (Col. 1:28–29).

In our pastoral labor, Christ is the message and Christlikeness is the goal. We want those in our care to be conformed to Christ, which happens as faith works through love. So the goal of a pastor in all his labor is to elicit faith in Christ through the proclamation of his gospel message. This is true in public as well as personal proclamation of the Word. Faith reframes the heart's functions so that a person once animated by sinful desire, darkened thinking, and earthly loyalties is ever-increasingly animated by righteous desire, enlightened thinking, and heavenly loyalties. And the only way faith emerges in the heart is through the ears hearing the message proclaimed: "So faith comes from hearing, and hearing through the word of Christ" (Rom. 10:17).

Pastoral labor requires speaking to people on behalf of God in Christ. Paul was so committed to growing believers in Christ that if believers failed to persevere in faith, Paul said his labor would have been in vain (Phil. 2:16; see also Gal. 4:11). Establishing faith was the central goal of all his labors.

Proclaiming Christ requires pastors to go to the dark places in people's lives—those off-putting problems that are simply easier to ignore than to address. It could be marriages that are showing signs of fragmentation, alarming patterns in the life of a teen, disunity between two longtime members, the plaguing doubts of a church staffer, the mental volatility of a young man. Whatever the complexity of people's troubles, you can always ask yourself this orienting question: What does faith in Christ look like in this person's trouble?

Jesus needs to be proclaimed in those dark places. And the pastor must not be afraid to go there. It is true—many of the issues that will confront you in personal ministry are beyond your experience and your ability to handle adequately. But keep in mind two things.

First, as with everything in life, your skill in navigating the dark places is developed only *by practice*. A pastor will grow in his abilities only as he humbly takes on the task of caring closely for people. Sure, he will make plenty of mistakes along the way—from presuming to understand too much to failing to speak authoritatively out of fear of their response. But mistakes are a necessary part of improvement. The key to minimizing damage is humility. Serve people with the Word and recognize the limits of your perspective. Just how you serve people is what we'll unpack in the coming chapters. Our main point here is simply that fear of failure must not keep you from going into the dark places.

Be assured that you will grow along the way. You will pick up on the subtleties of interpersonal dynamics, assessing trouble, leading a person to recognize patterns of thought or desire, and processing situations in biblically helpful ways. As with a hardwood tree, your growth will be mostly imperceptible when it's happening. But when you look back over months and years, it will be undeniable.

Second, and even more important, your confidence for navigating the dark places is not in you in the first place, but in Christ. Remember the passage that opened our discussion; the goal of ministry is Christ. But remember: the *means* of ministry is also Christ. "For this I toil, struggling with all his energy that he powerfully works within me" (Col. 1:29). The source of Paul's energy is Christ, and his supply of it is powerful. This is the ground of our confidence and the only reason we would dare to wade into the dark waters of human trouble.

Ultimately, your confidence does not rest on your skill set, no matter how developed. Instead, your confidence is in the power of the gospel of Jesus Christ through the proclamation of his Word. What goes for the pulpit goes for the counseling room. In one sense, it was easier to be Spirit-dependent in our early days of preaching since we were so aware of our weakness. As we grow in skill, both exegetically and homiletically, we more easily forget our dependence upon the Lord to speak through his Word. Of course, this could happen in counseling as well, but that might be hard for you to imagine right now. But any sense of inadequacy in counseling should not be reason to avoid it; rather, it should keep you dependent upon God to do what he alone can do.

So, pastor, there is no need to fear the unknown. If you've arranged your pastoral ministry to avoid regular missions into the jagged and rocky places in people's lives, then you are not shepherding like Jesus. The grimy, sweat-streaked face of a pastor is but an image of that blood-streaked face we all love.

TWO

Where Do
We Begin?

"I need help," is the sheepish admission that often starts the process of pastoral counseling. The pastor, standing at the back door after Sunday morning service, instinctively knows that the hushed tone means something. He pauses the conversation as he does a quick mental calculation of what to do. "I wonder what's wrong? What should I do to help? Where do we begin?" He knows that every quiet confession can lead to a wide range of issues, from simple to complex.

INITIAL GOALS

Before we begin describing the process of counseling, it helps to keep a few overarching goals in mind. Remembering these throughout the process will also prevent you from going astray or lacking direction. To use a building metaphor, they are like the construction drawings that show what needs to be accomplished. There are three simple goals in offering pastoral counsel.

Address the Presenting Problem

First, and perhaps most obvious, we want to address the problem. Counseling is by nature problem-oriented. Like all other ministries, it is Christ-centered and Word-driven, but counseling typically comes about as a response to some area of trouble. The regular ministries of the Word are like gas stations and oil-change centers—they fuel and maintain your vehicle. But when the Ford breaks down, you take it to the shop. So also Christians who sit under the preaching of the Word week to week do not usually visit the pastor's office until something is wrong in their lives.

Pastors get to help struggling people respond wisely to their problems: anger needs control (Eph. 4:26); sorrow needs comfort (2 Corinthians 1); fear needs rest (Ps. 56:3–4). Couples in debt need budget goals and financial restraint; teenagers who cut themselves need behavioral strategies to stop; professionals addicted to pain pills need medical attention. Pastors have to tackle problems practically. People need thoughtful advice for real-life struggles.

But practical strategies by themselves are not enough. Counseling that is truly Christian will have much more: the person and work of Christ will be its theological and practical center. Christ and his gospel must be the foundation, means, and end of our counseling. If by the end of your time together you have not helped this person look more like Christ, then what you've done is not Christian counseling. This leads to our second goal.

Display the Relevance of the Gospel

Second, we want the person to see the relevance of the gospel. People live right only when they are made right through Christ. Their deepest values, their hidden longings, and their understanding of the world, when not aligned with God's, will result in continual frustration and dysfunction. Their perspective on the problem will likely be flat-out earthly.

But the gospel is relevant because it reframes all earthly trouble with an eternal perspective. The Word of God exposes the heart in ways nothing else can, surgically bringing to light what is unhealthy (Heb. 4:12–13) so that what is out of order may be put right (Heb. 12:12–14). Faith is the means by which a person receives the righteousness of Christ, such that the quality and character of one's heart and life are transformed (Rom. 1:16–17; 6:22–23). Even when faith in the word of Christ is difficult, a person will always find Christ more than trustworthy with his or her life (Mark 9:24).

We need to rely on the gospel like this throughout our lives. The gospel is always relevant, and one of your goals as a counselor is to make this fact as apparent as possible. You do this by exposing the self-reliant lies we all tell ourselves: "I can fix this on my own." "Maybe this gospel stuff is helpful at church, but it won't make a real difference where I need it most in life." "If Christ loved me, he'd make this problem go away." "This is just too hard. I give up and don't care anymore."

The pastor should toss a grenade into the middle of such thinking. He must insist that problems in life are occasions for troubled persons to hear the beckoning voice of Christ, neither insisting on their own solutions nor giving up in hopelessness. None of these things will accomplish the greater gospel reliance that God desires in the hearts of those he loves.

3. Help People to Grow in Christlikeness

Third, and most important, we want to help people to grow to be more like Christ (Eph. 4:22–24; 5:1). Human beings were created to image God. The more we are conformed to his image, the closer we reflect God's ideal for human life (Rom. 8:29–30). As a person is sanctified, he will put off soul-withering pursuits and put on those that aim at Christlikeness. Remember, Christ is both the means and the goal of counseling.

We realize that this third goal may not initially sound all that helpful to someone in the throes of depression or trying to recover from the death of her child. Your challenge as a pastor is to show others in compelling ways why this goal—a life conforming to Christ—is much better than their immediate desire for happiness or release from grief. While we certainly labor for the depressed to have lightened spirits and the grieved to find relief, we don't stop there. We want them to see the glories of pursuing and becoming more like Christ. For believer and unbeliever alike, a pastor's counsel is simple: to be like Christ is to be most alive (John 10:10).

Honestly, this makes the effectiveness of counseling harder to gauge. How do you precisely measure conformity to Christ? Certainly there are indicators in changed desires and behaviors, in different thought patterns and purified concerns. But it's not like painting a fence, where you can see the color of your progress and know exactly how much further you have to go. The main confidence of the pastor is that if a person belongs to Christ, God has pledged himself to the task of renewing him or her. This was the apostle Paul's reason for continuing his labors: ". . . being confident of this, that he who began a good work in you will carry it on to completion until the day of Christ Jesus" (Phil. 1:6). It is our reason as well.

THE INITIAL ALERT

Now that the goals are laid out, let's consider how counseling is normally initiated. Not all situations start the same way.

Counseling can certainly start with the struggling person seeking help, but it can also be initiated by a concerned friend or the pastor himself directly approaching someone who seems to need help.

Self-Initiated Counseling

Self-initiated counseling is usually the most natural way to start. When someone seeks a pastor for counsel, it is usually because he is aware of his need for help. The hesitant person contacts the pastor directly—a phone call on a Tuesday morning, a cryptic e-mail or text, a muted conversation at the rear door of the church. Whatever the issue, such conversations can usually be summarized in three words: "I need help."

With the conversation started, the pastor can explore why the person needs help. We'll consider this much more in later chapters. For now, it's sufficient to say that a pastor should commend anyone who seeks help. Even if you later discover that the presenting trouble has little to do with the actual problem, you can celebrate the God-given humility the person is demonstrating in recognizing his or her need for help.

In self-initiated counseling, a sheep has cried out to his or her shepherd for help. And the shepherd should display a joyful eagerness to care for this hurting sheep (1 Pet. 5:2).

wes

Friend-Initiated Counseling

Other counseling situations are initiated by friends or loved ones. A small-group leader alerts you to trouble in a member's life; one roommate approaches you about another's odd habits; a parent comes for help with a rebellious teenager. In our experience, the most frequent example of friend-initiated counseling is a wife seeking help for her husband. This is a great example to consider, since it displays both the advantages and potential disadvantages of initiating counseling for someone else.

The New Testament casts a positive vision for church members watching over one another's lives (Gal. 6:1–2; Heb. 3:12–13; James 5:19–20), including making pastors aware of the needs of their people so as to shepherd them best. It is right for a wife to approach a pastor if she is concerned with the spiritual state of her husband.

But the potential disadvantages warrant caution on the counselor's part. First, a concerned spouse may approach the situation from a skewed or otherwise limited perspective. This spouse will likely have contributed to the trouble in areas she is blind to. So the pastor should be aware that the concerned spouse will also need help having a biblical perspective. Proverbs 18:17 says,

> The one who states his case first seems right,
> until the other comes and examines him.

This bit of wisdom reminds the pastor that as he approaches the named partner, he has a lot of listening to do first. The pastor should initiate a genuine exploration with the spouse in question, not hand down foregone conclusions.

Second, the person approached will likely be less open to counsel than if he were the one initiating the conversation. The fact that he hasn't come forward might suggest he is not ready or willing to be helped, and any intrusion from the pastor based on a third-party tip-off will only make things worse. Very often, therefore, the best advice to the friend is that she encourage the potential counselee himself to initiate communication with the pastor, or at least ask the individual if the pastor could contact him.

When circumstances appear to warrant unsought intervention, you should approach the person patiently and resolved to point him to Christ. It is also usually best to be up front about who first approached you about the trouble. In most cases, you should simply make it clear to the concerned friend that you will be using her name and will defend her decision to intervene as the loving and biblical thing to do. Approaching someone on an anonymous tip does not treat the church as the church. Candor diffuses potential awkwardness early and gets things in the open more quickly.

In friend-initiated counseling, a fellow sheep has alerted the shepherd to the wanderings of another. And the shepherd should display wisdom in his approach to help.

Pastor-Initiated Counseling

Other counseling situations are initiated directly by pastors who see areas of trouble in their people's lives and seek them out. Though this is sometimes a little awkward, approaching someone to care for him is part of the pastoral mandate (Titus 2:15; Heb. 13:17). Exercise of pastoral authority should never be an opportunity to bully, cajole, argue, or manipulate. We've seen pastors who, out of an apparent desire for both purity and efficiency, approach people with such brusqueness that they are all but sure to respond poorly.

The pastor should approach others with a candor that is founded upon patience and love (1 Thess. 5:14). This takes courage as well as skill. Both are developed in the doing. So, pastor, do not shy away from this task as if the Great Shepherd were not himself with you. As you clothe yourself with humility and patience, you will compel the hearts of your people to seek the grace they aren't aware they need.

In pastor-initiated counseling, a shepherd discerns the wanderings of his sheep and seeks him or her out. Especially here, the shepherd should display patience and persistence as he seeks to help.

THE INITIAL CONTACT

Having established a need for closer pastoral attention, how should a pastor begin the process of counseling? The initial contact can be thought of as involving three things: preview, prioritization, and pursuit.

Preview

We almost always request a preview of the problem. This can be done formally or informally. Requesting a formal preview may involve sending counselees a Personal Background Form as a framework for locating their problem and summarizing their perspectives of it. We've included an example of this in appendix C, where you will also find access to a digital version. A preview can also be informal, simply asking folks to write up a paragraph or two about their problem.

A preview offers a number of advantages. The pastor is given time to mobilize resources before the first session. Maybe he will pull the name of someone who has more expertise on the problem, grab a book that would be helpful for the person to read, or involve another Christian who has gone through a similar struggle.

A preview also lets you pray about the person and the problem before you meet for counseling. We encourage pastors to develop a habit of praying during their morning quiet time for all the people they'll be meeting that day. It is a good way to avoid the danger of trying to help others in your own wisdom rather than depending on the wisdom the Lord provides (James 1:5–8).

An additional benefit of getting a preview is that it helps the counselee organize his or her thoughts before coming in. Often the person has put very little thinking into how to describe the problem; as he explains things in front of you, he is still sorting through the multitude of difficulties that plague him. Rarely have we had someone come in and summarize his life in a succinct, well-organized way. More often folks spew out verbiage for the pastor to clean up. "I struggle with this . . . my wife hates that . . . maybe I should think about this . . . they're always telling me that . . ." You don't notice the clock has ticked twenty minutes away before the flow tapers off. Having some grasp of the nature of the situation beforehand will help you organize what can be an onslaught of details.

Prioritization

As a pastor, you are already painfully aware of your finitude. You have only so much time and energy. We trust that God has burdened you to spend both for the good of his people. To do this most effectively, you have to prioritize what situations get greater portions of your time. Having previewed the situation, you'll be able to weigh a few factors.

Time required. Basic marital problems or behavioral issues may require less time than more complex troubles involving deeply rooted value systems or long-running patterns of behavior. We are not saying that a pastor should prioritize those situations that take the least amount of time. In fact, those that require more usually need the most attention. But a pastor should be aware of the likely time demands. Experience gives you a feel for timing.

Level of exploration required. Some troubles require a great deal of exploration of people's thinking and desiring, of their personal history or relational dynamics with others. Those that require more exploration should usually take priority. Those situations that are more straightforward can usually be handled by small-group leaders or other Christian friends who are willing and able to pursue them.

Level of urgency. Every situation is urgent to those making the request. But part of your job as pastor is helping people to see their troubles in the context of other people's needs. Some counseling requests are simply not all that urgent when compared with others. The wise pastor knows his time, that of his staff and fellow elders, and that of other skilled folks in his congregation. In less urgent situations, the pastor should not feel guilty spending only a single meeting in which he encourages counselees to pursue growth through the more regular ministries of the Word, at least until his counseling load lightens. We'll say more about utilizing the other ministries of the church in chapter 7.

Available gospel-oriented relationships. Another factor is the relationships available to the person in need of help. If there are few gospel-minded folks available to guide someone, then counseling should be a higher priority. A pastor should be eager to care for a person groping blindly with no guide. Sometimes, given circumstances beyond anyone's control, the person just doesn't have many faithful guides. The pastor should pursue this person not just for direct counseling, but also to connect him to the life of the body.

Pursuit

A final issue to consider in the initial meeting is how much you should continue to pursue someone in need. Admittedly, how much to pursue a person is one of the harder equations a pastor has to calculate. He has to weigh the urgency of the situation, the receptiveness of the person's heart, and the other needs in the congregation. This is especially difficult in friend- or pastor-initiated counseling, since few people are eager to be pursued. Yet, pursuit of uninterested people is often the call of the pastor. The skill lies in discerning how much to pursue, and different situations will warrant different styles of pursuit. Here are a few profiles to consider.

Those who are initially interested but bad at follow-through. Often in a tumult of conviction or desperation, people will reach out to a pastor for help. But then they'll be embarrassed and evasive when you follow up. You serve them by not letting them slip away. So be persistent and even a bit insistent for at least an initial meeting to get a lay of the land. Usually once folks get over their hesitation for that first meeting, they see the value of the process.

Those who are uninterested or busy. If only we could inject the desire for help into some people's hearts. It would make our job a lot easier. But since we can't do this, we need to be prepared to make our case for the importance of seeking help. Getting an initial session with someone is usually not difficult; but getting them to commit to more can be troublesome. And in some situations, a busy schedule makes it legitimately difficult for the person to commit. In these situations, it is best to approach people from the angle of priorities. If you were offering them an hourly wage of $1500 to meet with you, they would find the time as well as the interest. And what you offer from the Word is infinitely more valuable to their joy and well-being.

Those who are hostile. Even in churches, people are sometimes hostile toward leaders for various reasons. If that hostility is personal suspicion of a certain pastor, then we would advise the church's leaders to arrange meetings with a different pastor or staff member for ministry to this disgruntled individual. Part of the long-term care would be to seek reconciliation, of course. But trying to understand *why* a person is hostile is very important to the care of her soul. Hostility is a direct path to at least one major facet of her trouble. In situations where a person is hostile to the entire leadership of the church, it may be wise for those elders to seek help from pastors at another like-minded church.

Those who are overzealous. You may already know the feeling of getting numerous calls from the same individual in one day. The person's pursuit of you quickly becomes inappropriately intense, but you may feel guilty for even thinking so. Don't feel guilty. Part of loving people is helping to shape their expectations. It is always more merciful to lay down appropriate ground rules early than to allow people to overly depend on you. They must learn that the Lord is their constant refuge, and that you are his servant, among other servants, who will walk with them steadily over the long haul. And they must learn that all God's servants have limits.

With all of these situations, a pastor should avoid being too strong in pushing a counseling process on someone. Sometimes the Lord's timing is different from ours, and we can entrust such folks to him so long as we keep a close, caring eye on them. It may be that the Lord intends to let their trouble kick them around a bit more. Or, it may be the Lord's will to transform their hearts through some other means by which the Word penetrates their life. We should be humbly open to God, not insisting on the particular tool we think is most appropriate.

On the other hand, someone who is living in outright, identifiable sin and thus destroying himself and those around him should be required to commit to meeting with a pastor. If the individual refuses to do so, that refusal may speak to a broader refusal to repent of this sin, which can eventually provoke the later stages of church discipline.

UP NEXT: OUR METHOD

Now that we have some grasp of how counseling starts, we can establish our method of approach. This is the last aspect of what we're calling the *concept* of counseling. After that, we'll be ready to walk through the process.

THREE

Your Method: How You *Do* Counseling

You would never trust an author who claimed to teach a fully developed method of preaching in one short chapter. We are not claiming to do so with counseling. But you do need to have some framework for directing a counseling conversation. We have done our best to boil it down to its most necessary elements so you can have a clear sense of what you're doing. We laid out the three main goals of counseling: to address the problem, to display the relevance of the gospel, and to help people grow in Christlikeness. If you have these goals clearly in mind, you will have a much greater chance of saying something beneficial.

Pastors know they need to do more than simply find a more compassionate way of saying, "Stop it," or hand a person two verses and say, "Let me know how those work for you." Pastoral counseling involves at least three core elements: listening, considering, and then speaking. Pastors actively utilize these three aspects of counseling in order to uncover, weigh, and offer redemptive insights for the troubles in their people's lives.

THE METHOD

If the goals of counseling are like construction drawings, then the method is like the implementation plan for the phases of construction. You start with the foundation, move through structural framing, and end with the finish work.

Pastoral counseling follows a similar trajectory—you move from listening to considering to speaking.

- *You listen to the problem*—to understand the context of the person's life and troubles (Prov. 18:2, 13; James 1:19).
- *You consider heart responses*—how the person's heart is responding to God, to self, to others, and to circumstances (Prov. 20:5).
- *You speak truth in love*—in order to teach, comfort, warn, encourage, advise, and admonish as appropriate (2 Corinthians 1; Col. 3:16; 1 Thess. 5:14).

These three actions—listening, considering, speaking—are key to our methodology. All three parts are woven throughout the process of counseling.

1. Listen to the problem. You want to know what is going on, but people often share their troubles haphazardly, piling up details in an unorganized lump. You can sort things into smaller piles and help a person organize what he is saying. Here is a system of organization we've found helpful:

- *Circumstances.* First, what is going on? What circumstances seem most important to the person?
- *Other people.* Who are the most prominent people in his story? How are they treating him? How is he treating them?

- *Self*. What is his posture toward his troubles? Does he see himself as a victim, perpetrator, inferior, superior, ignorant, insightful, confused, clear-headed, guilty, innocent?
- *God*. How is the person factoring (or not factoring) God into his troubles? What is his perspective of the Lord's involvement with his predicament?

2. Consider heart responses. After you've found out the basics of what's going on, you want to consider how the person's heart is responding in each of these areas. His responses will be characterized either by faith or by a number of other things—fear, anger, discouragement, lust, indulgence, escape, ignorance, sadness, disappointment, discontentment, suspicion.

- *Circumstances*. Does the person recognize the difference between his circumstances and his *response* to his circumstances? Is his response characterized by faith or by something else?
- *Other people*. Is this person loving others? Is he being influenced by others in unbiblical ways?
- *Self*. What is this person's functional identity—the beliefs or values about himself that shape his conduct? How does this identity align with what God says about him in the gospel?
- *God*. Does this person trust God to be who he says he is and to do what he says he will do? Or is there some preferred version of God he's quietly holding?

3. Speak the truth in love. Speaking accurately to the need of the heart comes only after listening and considering. A pastor knows whether to teach, comfort, warn, encourage, advise, and admonish from Scripture based on the person's heart responses. The goal is to call people to faith in a way that specifically addresses their heart responses, since faith alone is the means by which a person responds rightly (Heb. 11:6, 13–16; 12:1–2). And faith comes through hearing the word of Christ (Rom. 10:17). This is why counseling must be biblical. Here are some appropriate ways you can speak to a person's need:

- *Circumstances.* A pastor gives biblical guidance appropriate to the situation. For those grieving, he comforts them by pointing to the hope found in God (Rom. 8:18–25). For the abused, he protects them from the abuser with the law (13:1–4) and calls them to forgive (Luke 6:27–36). For the anxious, he helps them understand that fear reveals desires that must be actively entrusted to a loving God (Phil. 4:4–13).
- *Other people.* A pastor will help people get a biblical vision of how to relate to others with both the dignity and humility of Christ. Active faith means loving others instead of fearing or using them (Rom. 13:8–10). You help people see what it means to believe the best about others while being realistic about their faults and sins (12:17–21). You help them know how to lay down personal interests for the sake of others (Phil. 2:1–8). ⌣ sc Christ ID Handout
- *Self.* A pastor calls people out of rival identities and into Christ as their source of identity. These identities are where people try to find life—as a successful businessman, a respected minister, a capable mother—so finding confidence in these is a direct competitor to confidence in Christ alone (Phil. 3:3–16).
- *God.* Most importantly, a pastor helps people to have a more accurate view of God from his Word. You help them to know and trust God as the only way for human life to be meaningful and to yield lasting change in the soul (Jer. 9:23–24; Col. 1:9–10).

Figure 1 illustrates this methodology of listening, considering, and speaking.

Figure 1.

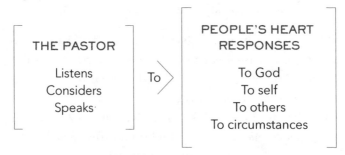

CONCLUSION

We have laid out the *concept* of counseling in these three chapters, beginning with a vision of counseling as pastoral labor, moving to the broad goals in counseling, and rounding it out with a description of the method of counseling. This gives you what you need now to understand the *process* you're going into, beginning with the initial meeting. Our hope is that if we can walk you through the shape of an entire counseling conversation, you will be better equipped to do it yourself.

A Few Practical Considerations for Your Office

- *Be prepared for the criers.* Have a box of tissues next to the couch or a chair where folks typically sit for counseling. Even with it there, someone who is emotionally overwhelmed might not notice the tissues, so you can serve criers with a simple prompt like, "There are tissues next to you."

- *Position clocks strategically.* Put a clock on the wall above the counseling couch or chair, within your natural line of sight. Avoid looking at your watch or cell phone during the session; it will make counselees feel hurried. Occasionally peek at the clock so that you can pace the session without making the person feel time-conscious.

- *Limit interruptions.* Don't take phone calls or check texts during your counseling sessions. In fact, silence your phone. If it does go off, reach over to silence it without diverting your eyes from the counselee.

- *Be visible at all times.* Your office door should feature a large, clear pane of glass for maximum visibility. Situate the counseling couch so that the counselee cannot be seen, but position your chair directly in the line of sight through the glass. And have someone (like a secretary at her desk) seated in the area just outside your office.

- *Put only recommended books on your shelves.* We should be regularly reading books we resonate with, as well as books we don't. But have only the books you'd recommend on the shelves of your counseling office. While folks are looking around, they'll take note of these titles and think, "That book looks helpful. And my pastor read it." So leave the bad books at home. That way there is no confusion about what you would and wouldn't recommend.

Part Two

PROCESS

FOUR

The Initial Meeting

If there were a competition to determine who dreads the first meeting most, the pastor would probably win. As nervous as a guy coming for help probably is at the thought of divulging personal struggles, the pastor is probably more nervous about hearing them. He's the one who's supposed to have the answers that will bring life—or at least, not too much death.

In the midst of such anxiety, the pastor can respond in some unhelpful ways. For one, he can dread counseling so much that his main goal becomes getting through it. So he comes up with a list of loosely related questions to fill the time. Or he can shrug off the pressure by finding a book on his shelf or a passage of Scripture to talk about the entire time. Maybe he does an awkward combination of the two.

We have laid out the three main goals of counseling (chapter 2): to address the problem, to display the relevance of the gospel, and to help people grow in Christlikeness. These were like construction drawings. We then thought through your preparation for the first meeting (chapter 2). We've also given the method of attaining the main goals of counseling (chapter 3).

This preparation and methodology is like the block foundation on which the whole enterprise will rest.

Now that we've established the method behind the counseling process, let's see how this unfolds in the initial meeting. This initial meeting is not necessarily the first step in a months-long journey. Most pastors won't be able to see someone for an extended period of months or years. With a packed schedule, the demands of preaching, and the need to preserve time for their families, most pastors will maintain a short-term model of pastoral care. When someone comes to the pastor, one to five meetings is fairly normal, six to ten sessions is possible though less common, and more than ten is unusual. Though short-term, this model can be quite effective, especially when wedded with the regular ministries of the Word, both public (preaching, teaching, singing, praying) and more personal (community groups, fellowship, one-on-one discipleship).

The initial meeting primarily involves a lot of listening, the first point listed in our trajectory. But telling you to listen well is only so helpful, so here are four more specific goals in your initial counseling session. These goals often overlap and shouldn't necessarily be thought of as distinct steps.

ESTABLISH A RELATIONAL CONNECTION

First, establish a relational connection. When a person comes into the office, it's a good idea to greet him or her with an upbeat conversation about the normal things of everyday life. This is easiest with someone you know already, but not impossible with someone you don't. Maybe it's the joys and pains of his job, how her weekend went, the latest news, or tomorrow's big game. Small talk goes a long way in helping folks sense that their problems are not the defining factor of life.

But the pastor bears the responsibility of transitioning to weightier matters. You can start with an opener, like "How can I help you today?" or, if you've done your prep work, "I had a chance to look through what you sent me and pray for you. How are you doing with everything?" It doesn't have to be fancy. Transition *out of* small talk and *into* the counseling conversation with a simple and straightforward question.

As you do this, keep in mind that you are seeking to establish the four most important commodities of any pastoral counseling relationship: trust, mercy, love, and respect. These are the basic building blocks for any counseling conversation.

Trust. In some ways, trust is the liquid gold of counseling. Without it, nothing else will move forward. While you might hope that the pastor has earned the general trust of a member because of his public ministry, you will find in counseling that, as in any other relationship, personal trust must be earned. Most folks come into counseling with a mixture of hopefulness and skepticism. They are open to the pastor because of what they have seen of him in his ministry, but they are also a bit skeptical because they're not yet sure he's going to receive them and guide them competently. A major part of earning trust is showing humility by listening well and speaking with consideration. No one trusts an arrogant know-it-all. On the other hand, a major part of earning trust is also in displaying confidence— not confidence in self, but in God's ability to give the wisdom needed for any trouble. The pastor's disposition to the trouble should be compassionate but composed. People will usually see such confidence for what it is—not self-assured arrogance, but humble confidence in God.

Mercy. When people come with their problems, they're usually tender and quick to feel judged. Most of the time, they are aware that something they're doing is wrong, even if they aren't willing to consider the extent. This makes their radar for condemning words very sensitive. If they sense condemnation—in words, in tone, in body language—you won't get anywhere. Sometimes their sensitivity is turned up so high it's basically impossible for them not to interpret you as condemning. But with a careful display of patience, the pastor can usually deconstruct a defensive wall. Having a merciful disposition is not merely a communication strategy; if that's all it is, it will quickly wear thin. Rather, it must be the emanation of a heart that is like God's—big with mercy, eager for the redemption of foolish, lost, or hostile people.

You will definitely see your share of foolishness—sometimes baffling foolishness. As folks share honestly about their thoughts and desires, their reasoning, and their behavior, you will often sense (usually accurately) just how dumbed with sin they've become. The list is endless: self-harm, suicidal thoughts, destructive communication, alcohol and drug addictions, pride and selfishness, hatred, jealousy, backstabbing. In those moments, you pray to have the heart of the Father who took on the shame of his wayward son rather than the heart of the older brother who trumpeted that shame (Luke 15:11–32). It is no exaggeration, dear pastor, to say that what God did for you in Christ was to take a perverted fool and give him the righteous wisdom of his own Son. Don't forget that. Remember God's mercy to you, and you will be ready to show mercy to the sinner who sits in front of you. More than a few people have told us after an initial counseling session, "I came here expecting condemnation, not mercy." ← Goal

Love. As with mercy, the source of love is God. "We love because he first loved us" (1 John 4:19). "Beloved, if God so loved us, we also ought to love one another" (4:11). Part of God's plan to display his love to a languishing world is to embody that love in a Christian's care and acceptance of other believers. The apostle John appeals to the fact that God is invisible, beyond the immediate detection of our senses. But you are not. As you embody this love, you make it tangible. John says, "No one has ever seen God; if we love one another, God abides in us and his love is perfected in us" (4:12). <u>Pastors have the privilege of making an invisible God visible to struggling people as they show Christlike love.</u>

Loving someone means showing concern for his well-being, even if you are unable to fix his particular troubles. That kind of love is actually more important than a solution. So if you are prone to fix things, be warned. No one likes to be a project. Be more committed to a person's well-being than to solving a problem. The two are actually not the same.

Don't Be Mr. FixIt

Respect. You will find yourself frequently sitting across from people who are total messes. They know it. You know it. And they know you know it. The pastor is called to show respect *(honor)* to people even in such a state. Honestly, this is difficult when dealing with folks who are shifty, egocentric, foolish, arrogant, or just plain infantile. Even in these cases, a pastor can maintain a level of respect by acknowledging every person as a divine image bearer (Gen. 1:26–28) who is a potential image bearer of God's very own Son (Rom. 8:29; 2 Pet. 3:9). All people, therefore, are invested with the dignity of reflecting God, no matter how warped or dimmed that image has become.

<u>Showing respect means being approachable.</u> We've all met pastors who aren't. That's a big problem. Self-righteousness and judgmentalism slowly decay the heart of a public teacher, and that rot will quickly stink. The scent of superiority rather than

humility is a stench to Jesus, since it is the opposite of his example (Phil. 2:5–8). One way to consider other people's interests as more important than your own is to show the respect of taking them seriously.

EXPLORE THE CONCERN

Too many of us assume we are good listeners when in fact we are not. Many pastors struggle to have patience to really listen to the people who come for help. We must avoid the pastoral temptation to turn every counseling session into another sermon. In counseling, pastors listen first and speak second. We must heed Solomon's warning:

> A fool takes no pleasure in understanding,
>> but only in expressing his opinion. (Prov. 18:2)

The central goal of the first meeting is to understand the person and his primary concerns. Getting to know people—how they respond to life, what they most value, how they relate to others, and so on—is what God has called you to do in reflecting his own concern for them. This is where the method we laid out in chapter 3 comes in handy.

We believe it is usually best to open with a general question that allows the person to direct the conversation in the way that seems most pressing to him. Above we suggested saying something like, "How can I help you today?" This, of course, does not mean the person will set the agenda for the entire meeting; it only means you are letting him discuss what he is most concerned about.

Listening well requires the delicate balance between allowing someone freedom to roam and keeping the person in the correct field. We are all inclined differently. Some of us tend to be such passive listeners that we never interject a helpful question to direct things. We may let struggling counselees take the lead when, frankly, they don't know where to go. Others may be inclined to keep the conversation as efficient as possible by directing it with a strict agenda of directing questions. The counselee feels led by the nose and is probably less likely to give needed information. Listening in such a way that helpfully directs the conversation is a tough skill to master.

Think of it in terms of fencing the conversation, but not leashing the person. You want individuals to feel freedom to go where they want to within the proper boundaries, but not to feel forced along a specific path. Patiently listen and don't talk over counselees, but at the same time, don't be passive. More than likely, you've got only an hour or so. If you let them talk about whatever they want at whatever pace they want, they will probably mention some useful things, but many less useful things. The key is to ask follow-up questions that will give you useful information. This is showing them the fence without leashing them too tightly. An excellent follow-up question will both acknowledge a person's concern and direct the conversation toward the most helpful information in getting to the bottom of the problem.

In order to ask good follow-up questions, you need to be clear about what kind of information you're looking for. Ask questions that direct you to heart issues, not just superficial details. Use the categories of the method we laid out in chapter 3 as fence lines. Basically, you are seeking to discern how a person's heart is responding to God, self, other people, and circumstances.

Go beyond questions that collect superficial data on a person's life. Of course you need enough details about your friend's life to understand the larger context for his or her problem, but there is danger in not going beyond this. We are more prone to collect lots of factual data about someone's life than to ask questions that pursue any depth. Depth questions are *heart-related* questions. They're harder to ask because they're intrusive. They attempt to expose who a person is (Prov. 4:23; 20:5; Matt. 12:34; Luke 6:43–45). Pursuing someone's heart helps you to understand the thoughts, desires, cravings, and motives that lie behind the behavior. It's no casual conversation.

We encourage you to take notes in order to help you stay focused on the conversation. Taking notes also helps you to organize the data a person rattles out with little concern for organization. Appendix D describes a simple method for taking notes and organizing data. Notes help an overburdened mind remember things accurately.

DISPLAY HOPE

One of your primary jobs this first session is to display hope to someone who's probably pretty hopeless. The hope you display should not be simply that things will get better in his or her situation. We certainly pray to this end, but know that the Lord Jesus uses trials to accomplish great things in the lives of those who trust him.

This is a great time to get a person looking at Scripture. Be sure to open your Bible during the first meeting. If God's Word really matters to the process of change, you need to show it. But how you use Scripture is just as important as the fact that you're using it. Fundamentally, you want a person to see his life from God's perspective, which means that you, the pastor, need a sound approach to Scripture. An imprecise hermeneutic is like a blind man with a big gun. There is simply too much power there to handle it poorly.

A thorough hermeneutics lesson is outside the scope of this little book. What we want to stress most is that Scripture's central concern is the glory of God displayed in the person and work of Jesus Christ. God's Word addresses all human problems only in light of that. Its relevance, authority, and sufficiency mean that what the Bible emphasizes as most important in human life, we emphasize as most important in human life. So for a depressed individual, we want her to feel better, but this is not our central concern. Rather, her depression should serve as an opportunity to reframe her perspective on life to center on eternal hopes. These eternal hopes will, in turn, reshape the way she feels about her present life.

So display hope by using the broad color scheme of Scripture to paint a vision of this person's life in light of cosmic glory. One way to do this is to conclude your initial session by summarizing what you heard from your counselees about their trouble and adding what the Bible says is possible regarding it. All hope ultimately rests in the finished work of Christ, so you can't go wrong with basic texts that display this life-transforming hope (Rom. 15:13; Eph. 1:18–19; Col. 1:21–23; 1 Tim. 4:10; Titus 3:5–7; 1 Pet. 1:3–5). But you can also focus on specific aspects of that hope that tailor to their specific situations. For example:

Key

- In situations of great suffering, the hope of a redeemed creation (Rom. 8:18–25)
- In situations of grief, the hope of God's sorrow-ending presence (Rev. 21:1–5)
- In situations of conflict, the hope of God's peace between warring parties (Eph. 2:14–18)
- In situations of distrust in God, the hope of his reception of honest expressions of faith (Lam. 3:1–25)

These are just a few examples. The point is that you can instill hope not only with passages that include the term *hope*, but also with any passage of Scripture that demonstrates the character of God displayed in the gospel of Jesus Christ. So the nuances of hope are as plentiful as the aspects of God's character: his redemptive intention toward resistant people, his ability to change any heart to respond in life-giving ways, his wisdom in arranging the meticulous details of every day, his kindness toward the weak and hurting, his justice in one day righting every wrong, his fierceness in protecting his children. We could go on. The point is that true hope is hope in God. And you help struggling people by giving them some concrete aspect of God's character to hope in, one that is appropriate to their need.

SET EXPECTATIONS

As you draw to a close, you'll want to hit a few housekeeping matters to help set healthy expectations. First, assign prep work. Part of the counseling process occurs outside the meeting. To borrow language from 1 Peter 1:13–14, this homework is part of preparing the mind for action, of setting hope on the grace of Christ, and of compelling a soul away from evil desire. Personal effort is a necessary part of preparing the soul for growth.

Given that prep work is an important part of guiding a soul toward Christ, a major component of prep work is Scripture. Basically, you want to give pertinent passages of Scripture with questions that will help guide individuals to how it applies to their life situation. The Scripture you set before a person should never be the result of a reckless search of the Bible for quick, trite answers. You should present passages for study in a way that will help someone see how their heart can relate rightly to Christ in troublesome circumstances.

Here are some guiding questions for determining what passages would be helpful:

- What does this person need to see more clearly about the Lord Jesus? About his gospel?
- What does this person need to understand better about him- or herself?
- What does this person need to hear about how to relate to others?
- How can this person's perspective on life be adjusted by a biblical view of suffering?

Frame the passage with helpful questions that will guide the person to these insights. These questions should not be too complex, but rather should be a basic guide to principles in the text that are pertinent to the trouble at hand. Here's an example:

> Take a moment to read Psalm 13. There the psalmist is experiencing some circumstantial trouble, but he processes this trouble primarily from the perspective of God "hiding his face" (v. 1). How can you relate this to the loss of your job? What does the psalmist request of God (v. 3)? In your situation, do you think the Lord Jesus would hear a similar request? What does the psalmist determine to do, having offered his request (vv. 5–6)? What might it look like for you to do the same with all the fear, shame, and anger that are gripping you from this loss?

To be able to do this well, you simply have to know your Bible. And the more you experience both the comfort and discomfort found in its pages, the more you'll be able to sense what is appropriate for another person. In addition to Scripture reading and prayer, other helpful types of assignments may be

- reading a pertinent book, with guiding questions;
- a relational exercise, such as writing a letter to someone;
- a responsibility exercise, which outlines a person's duties in relation to God or other people;
- a conflict exercise, in which a couple processes the dynamics of a fight, using guiding questions;
- journaling;
- writing out a prayer of praise, confession, or thanksgiving.

Our hope is that through prep work, we teach the person to rely on God's Word. Nothing can substitute for this. Other forms of prep work should always be complements to the central task of Scripture intake and prayerful meditation.

A second housekeeping matter, as you wrap up, is to take a moment to trace out the parameters for the counseling relationship. Regarding duration, the pastor will have to gauge as well as he can how much counseling is needed and give at least a rough estimate of how many more meetings can be expected. Avoid the impulse to overpromise. If you're not sure, then just say you'll revisit the topic at the next meeting. Also, be clear how long each session will last. For instance, if you plan to meet weekly, then keeping meetings to one hour is a good discipline to maintain for the benefit of both pastor and counselee. If meetings are more spread out—like once a month—then you might consider ninety minutes or more.

Regarding contact outside of scheduled meetings, a pastor needs to be careful to set appropriate boundaries to protect his family as well as his own soul. Weak sheep have the remarkable ability to find the gaps in a pastor's boundaries. We could retire in Bermuda if we had a dollar for every phone message that started with, "I know you're with your family, but . . ." It's best to give clear guidelines on what is and isn't an appropriate time to call, how long it may take to return messages, and what constitutes an emergency. One of our rookie pastoral mistakes was offering couples in bad marriages the opportunity to call us whenever they were in a nasty fight. Guess what happened? We got calls at all hours of the night, and with ridiculous frequency. So unless you enjoy buzzing phones on your night stand, have the conversation.

The final thing to do before concluding in prayer is to get the next meeting penciled in on your calendar. After the first meeting is done and everyone has gone back to the hustle and bustle of everyday life, a lot of time and energy can be wasted in tracking people down and coordinating calendars via e-mail or texts or phone calls. So the easiest thing to do is to coordinate schedules while everyone is present at the initial meeting.

Then, do pray for them. Not perfunctorily, but with unhurried sincerity. You want to model for them heartfelt interaction with the living God about their particular problem. Do your best to avoid statements they would be tempted to dismiss as trite. As you pray through each of the problems, pray in a way that shows them how the gospel is a sufficient answer to their troubles and how they can draw near to the throne of grace to receive help in time of need.

FIVE

Laboring for Change

Any builder will tell you that a quality foundation gives confidence that the next steps will bring about a successful build. So it is with counseling. The initial sessions we've covered so far serve only as a starting point for building into the life of a person. You still have a ways to go in following the implementation plan. At every stage, remember the method we laid out of listening, considering, and speaking to the way the heart responds to God, to others, to circumstances, and to self.

In this chapter, we hope to teach you how to keep the counseling process moving. If we only perpetuate the things we were doing in the initial sessions, we merely overbuild the foundation, and nothing useful is created. Erecting a structure requires a different set of tasks and skills.

This next stage covers the bulk of your meetings. You may still be covering material from your initial session, and that's normal. We are not implying a hard shift into some other task in these next sessions, but a gradual emergence. In this chapter we will unpack four key elements that should be part of each session in this next stage to a greater or lesser degree: (1) get an update; (2) ask about prep work; (3) continue to explore the concern; (4) offer redemptive remedies.

GET AN UPDATE

First, get an update. You want to have a strong sense of what is most pressing on a person's mind when he or she comes in the room. Often people are annoyed about a conversation they've just had, dread having to admit to some failure from the last week, or worry about some situation that just arose at work. Asking for an update on how they are doing allows them to express what is most pressing to them. This can provide golden insight into how a person's heart is actively responding to present circumstances. It can also be a wonderful opportunity to show the relevance of the Bible to situations that at first blush don't seem all that spiritually significant. The Bible has jurisdiction over everything in life, and you show this by being concerned with a person's immediate experience.

You want the questions to be simple and open-ended, but with an element of direction. Here are a few suggestions, all of which are slight variations that get at the same thing:

- Give me an update on how things went this week regarding some of the issues we've discussed.
- How are you doing with all this—discouraged or encouraged?
- Do you have any new thoughts or realizations over the last week or so?
- Have any situations come up that are related to what we've been talking about?
- Has anything happened this week that you think would be helpful to talk through?

Sometimes what comes up from these general questions is important enough to redirect the trajectory of a session because you sense a compelling need to address a particular issue. Other times, they will simply help you get to know the person better. Either way, updates are not just a polite way of getting to the main part of a counseling session. They are important for understanding the immediate experience of someone so that you can counsel with an eye on the current state of the person's heart and life.

ASK ABOUT PREP WORK

Asking about previously assigned prep work should immediately follow the opening update. Checking on homework doesn't turn you into a schoolmarm. Rather, you're exploring how the material compelled a person to understand his own heart better and to see Christ amid his trouble.

The most common assignment given between sessions will be the study of a relevant Bible passage and prayerful meditation. You should take time to explore the assigned text and the biblical insights gained by the counselee. The best way to frame this is to ask questions that reveal three things:

1. Does the person understand what the text actually means?
2. Does he see the implications of that meaning for his life?
3. Does he see how those implications relate to Christ Jesus?

Basically, reviewing prep work is a good way to teach a person to read the Bible well and to entrust himself to its real-life wisdom.

If other assignments were given (journaling, worksheets, practical exercises, and so on), be sure to check on those assignments and what the person got out of them. If you don't ask about the prep work, you show that you don't think it's all that important. Your counselee will quickly agree with you and lose motivation to do it.

When folks don't do the work, don't jump on them. Some folks find life so overwhelming they can't get much else done, and the prep work you assigned was unrealistic in light of those challenges. We don't know too many deeply depressed people who will read a full-length book or moms of toddlers who can have extended times of prayer and Scripture meditation. Know the challenges of the person's life so you can give appropriate prep work. Of course, it's possible that someone is only interested in using counseling sessions to gripe and complain but is unwilling to actually do something about the problem. If a person demonstrates a consistent lack of follow-through, then it's time to have a conversation about not wasting his time or yours with a process that isn't actually proceeding.

CONTINUE TO EXPLORE THE CONCERN

If your prep work is set up well, talking about it will lead naturally into exploring the known areas of concern a bit more. In the bulk of the sessions, you continue to grow in your understanding of counselees' problems by watching how their hearts respond to the latest happenings. Life continues to unfold for them. Observe it. Bad marriages will dissolve. Ladies with eating disorders will lose more weight. Depressed people will miss work. Cutters will cut. The point is, problems are never static. You're trying to understand how a person's heart is actively responding to what is currently unfolding.

People's situations evolve over time, and the pastor will need to keep up. It is not always easy to keep the facts of a person's situation distinct from her responses to the situation. You have to listen carefully to the language people use—it may be charged with emotion, reveal some critical misperception, divulge some unhealthy loyalty. Words have a barometric pressure to them. They reveal what a person believes, what she desires, and what she is dedicated to. "I hate my husband." "I don't think God cares for me." "I give up." "No one knows what it's like." These statements reveal both beliefs and emotions. Don't be scared to face either. If you shy away from topics that reveal stronger emotions, you'll miss a tremendous opportunity to gauge the heart. Don't awkwardly rush through emotional moments. Often such times bring you closest to finding a person's deepest longings and beliefs. These moments can get you closer to the pivotal question of what this someone worships. Are the person's values and beliefs geared toward the worship of Christ Jesus, or are they used in service to self?

The categories of a person's heart responses (to God, to self, to others, to circumstances) that we laid out in our method provide a way of gauging what a person worships. God's image bearers were made to worship. That natural drive to worship will be directed at God or a thousand rival gods: the affirmation of social acceptance, the satisfaction of professional accomplishments, the security of a certain relationship, the comfort of an easier lifestyle. What people tend to talk about, who they are attracted to, how they spend their time—in summary, how their hearts respond to life—are matters of worship. Pastors should think of counseling not primarily as an attempt to fix problems, but as an attempt to reorient worship from created things to the Creator by means of the gospel of Jesus Christ.

Here are two important cautions when exploring a person's situation and heart responses. First, don't be hasty or simplistic in labeling what a person's heart is worshiping. You are not on an idol hunt, as if these things could be easily labeled. A thirty-four-year-old addicted to video games is not worshiping his Xbox. A sexually active teen is not worshiping her boyfriend. Like the Canaanite fertility gods that Israel was so drawn toward, these objects are typically means of attaining something else. Israel was enamored not with a carved piece of wood, but with what they thought that god could grant them: fertility, wealth, prosperity, safety, belonging, generational perpetuity—in other words, life on their own terms. All of these benefits they wanted apart from the Creator of them. So Israel's true problem was that they rejected God to pursue life apart from him.

The video-game addict is using the Xbox as an object to attain a number of possibilities: the significance of doing great deeds, an escape from the difficulties of real existence, or the simple pleasure of impulse stimulation. Whatever the combination, he is seeking life apart from God's rule. The sexually active teen is using her boyfriend to attain a number of possibilities herself: a sense of relational belonging, acceptance in a peer group, escape from an unloving family, maybe the simple pleasure of sex. These are worship issues that go deeper than the surface object.

Second, when a person comes to you for help, don't assume he is fully conscious of what motivates him. People can have motives, desires, and even beliefs they are not fully conscious of. Not every aspect of a person's response is the result of immediate, conscious determination. We are not necessarily agreeing with the theory of a subconscious prevalent in many psychologies. We are simply pointing out that people have different degrees of awareness of their desires, beliefs, or intentions. Counseling often grows a person's insight into his own heart, helping him to be more aware of why he thinks, feels, or acts in certain ways.

Why are we even mentioning this second caveat? It keeps us from simply defaulting to admonishing people. Often, direct exhortation is not the place to start. An angry husband may think he is simply ticked over whatever the last fight was about—say, a disagreement about finances. Simply identifying his idol as money and chastising him for his anger will not do. You have to help him become more aware of things he believes about his wife (that she is materialistic or disrespectful), of things he wants (freedom to do as he pleases), and of other ways his anger expresses itself (sarcastic comments, a lack of warmth toward her).

What this man needs is patient instruction and exploration that will illumine his heart. This takes time. You don't want to simply tell him what his idols are then admonish him to worship God instead. Don't assume people are fully conscious of what motivates their feelings and behavior. Admonition is necessary, but it is most effective when someone becomes aware of both *what* he is doing and *why* he is doing it.

These important caveats about how to address a worshiping heart will help you to handle people in ways appropriate to where they are. The apostle Paul states in 1 Thessalonians 5:14, "And we urge you, brothers, admonish the idle, encourage the fainthearted, help the weak, be patient with them all." Paul encourages us to be discerning in our approach to people with differing problems. Idle folks need warning. Timid folks need encouragement. Weak folks need help. The faithless need hope. The foolish need rebuke. The abused need safety. The grieving need comfort. And the list could go on.

The one constant in every counseling conversation is being

"patient with everyone." Spiritual growth takes time, and that requires patience in both counselor and counselee. Keep in mind the bigger picture and the longer view. Counseling may only last for a few meetings, but spiritual growth should be pursued over a lifetime (Phil. 1:6; 2:12–13). Our overarching goal is to build spiritual infrastructure in lives, not just to plug leaking dams. As people's awareness of their hearts grows, so can their faith in Christ, so that they become more Christlike with every passing day.

OFFER REDEMPTIVE REMEDIES

Finally, offer redemptive remedies. At some point in every counseling conversation there should be a shift from exploring the concern to providing specific guidance for the person's problems. Once you are updated, have reviewed the prep work, and have explored the concern a bit more, it's time to move into a conversation about the best ways to deal with the problems.

Much of your work in the last step was uncovering how the heart is worshiping. In this next step, we are encouraging a person to worship God in her specific situation. How is she responding to the difficulties in her life? Does she have faith in God, or has she placed her hope elsewhere? No strategy a pastor employs can induce a person to worship. Only God can compel worship in the heart. And though there is much mystery here, a few things are clear in Scripture:

- Rightly relating to God in worship occurs only by faith (Rom. 1:16–32).
- Faith comes through hearing the word of Christ (Rom. 10:17).
- The word of Christ is proclaimed by human agents (Rom. 10:14–16).

Faith is a gift of God. But God chooses to use his people to proclaim his Word as the means of inciting faith. You can think of counseling as involving custom-built proclamation of God's Word as a means of building faith in Christ so that the heart can worship rightly. That's your goal: to promote faith that results in heart-felt, Christ-exalting worship regardless of the circumstances.

This does not mean that once you get a sense of the problem, you just start to preach at counselees rather than talking with them. Counseling is less like a sermon and more like a conversation. We've felt the same temptation you do in counseling—to tell people what's wrong with their lives and what God's Word says, and then usher them out the door. Please don't do that. Don't preach *at* them; talk *with* them.

But it is a conversation for the purpose of instruction. You are a pastor, after all. Study Scripture together, think of ways to apply it to their situations, and make concrete plans to commit to. Teach them from the text, especially when there is misunderstanding or bad interpretation. You may not realize that a fairly common complaint from those who go to professional counselors is not receiving enough guidance as to how to deal with their problems. Pastors should not make the same mistake. They should be channels of God's wisdom to suffering and sinning people.

Depending on the person and situation, the pastor can employ a host of redemptive strategies when suggesting a solution. Below are a few different strategies for helping someone see what responding in faith might look like in his or her situation. Please note: the following are not distinct steps, but rather a sampling of angles you can take for moving a person toward a solution.

Reintroduce God

Because of how rampant biblical illiteracy is in our day, it is not surprising that many Christians have a superficial understanding of the character of God. Yet knowing God as he reveals himself in his Word is the greatest source of confidence for human life (Jer. 9:23–24). Getting to know the character of God will prove helpful no matter what the problem.

A faulty understanding of God will affect how we respond to life. If a person sees God as critical and scrutinizing, she will respond with fearful resignation. Christianity becomes moral performance, and life becomes graceless. If a person sees God as a genie or Santa Claus, he expects God to grant him happiness. Not surprisingly, he will respond in frustration and disappointment when suffering comes and be miffed when you start talking in categories of God acting for his own ultimate glory.

Misconceptions of God are always tied to a person's deepest desires and core expectations of life. True knowledge of God brings order to these desires and expectations.

Depsychologize

Sometimes people have so embraced the culture's norms that a large part of your pastoral work is to dissuade them of priorities and values that simply are not biblical. Many of these folks will be self-professed Christians, yet view life largely from a framework of worldly standards. This can be explicit, such as overidentifying with psychological labels like various bipolar, depressive, or trauma-related disorders, or implicit, like when they speak in the language of pop psychology.

Helping someone to see him- or herself primarily as a child of God (rather than as bipolar or schizophrenic) or to accept suffering as normal for Christians (rather than run from it) is going to take patient reworking of some very subtle assumptions. The *truest* thing about a Christian is that he or she is the treasured possession of Christ, whatever may be going on physiologically. Until people operate out of this priority, they will struggle to respond to their trouble in faith (Phil. 4:3–16).

Deprogram Performance

If people are stuck in the performance trap—thinking they must "do" something in order to earn God's favor—then they need to grow in their understanding of free grace (Eph. 2:4–10) and learn to rest in God's love (Rom. 8:31–38). A lifetime of a legalistic performance mentality won't change overnight. Some church members will come to you so entrenched in a certain way of thinking and living that it will feel like you are deprogramming individuals who have just been sprung from a cult. Others will hide behind a legalistic view of God to prevent them from seeing the deeper ways they fall short. In either case, Christians who are deeply entrenched in unbiblical ways of thinking must be challenged with the dual truths that humans are far more shameful than any of us could bear to acknowledge, yet are able to be made far more holy than we could dare to hope.

Contrast Functional and Confessional Assumptions

What we say we believe and how we actually function are often quite at odds with one another. A grown woman who was beaten by her father as a child will have a hard time trusting men, let alone men in authority, despite knowing how Scripture describes the conduct of redeemed men. Or an adult who was essentially abandoned as a child by cocaine-addicted parents might walk around convinced that he has to fend for himself because no one else is going to, despite what he reads of the power of Christian fellowship. Both of these believers struggle with functional assumptions that act as guiding principles for their lives. In these two situations, the functional principles are fairly plain. Yet most of us walk around with much more subtle functional assumptions that misguide our lives, so they're trickier to identify.

Confessional assumptions, on the other hand, are what we know to be true according to the Bible. We can undermine bad functional assumptions by teaching true confessional assumptions (Ps. 73:1–28). Pastors need to root out the guilt, shame, and lies that define functional assumptions. And we must plead with, teach, and persuade the person of the amazing value of a life oriented to God's perspective. As the abused woman comes to terms with the abuse of her father and the love of God for her, she can reconsider whether loving, self-sacrificial male authority is actually possible this side of heaven. As the adult son of drug addicts learns about both the limits of and the redemption of human relationships in Christ, he will learn appropriate trust in others.

Reframe

A beautiful painting becomes compromised by a hideous frame. This is why purveyors of fine art are quite selective about their frames. So also, distress or fear can frame the way a person relates his life to you, conveying an overall picture of the situation that is unbearable. As a pastor, you can help people reframe the raw data of their lives with a distinctly biblical frame. Help the struggling person consider how God would frame his situation so that he can see the picture of his life a little more clearly.

A depressed man who thinks that his marital problems are

hopeless might be surprised at the pastor's perspective. His pastor has seen a lot of couples in distress, some in relationships similar to this man's marriage, and he knows a redemptive path is possible. The pastor's interpretation of the facts puts a new frame on the data that can provide new hope.

For your people's sake, don't accept their starting points or conclusions. Help them to consider other frames, other angles, other lighting that better draw attention to the redemptive hope in the picture. A reframing word is remarkably clarifying at times. This is the essence of encouragement—to *lend courage* in a situation. Paul did this with the Thessalonians by helping them frame their lives according to the glorious future that awaited them (1 Thess. 4:13–18).

Uncover Underlying Dynamics

In every situation, there are unspoken dynamics that define what is going on. A wife may have expectations for how money should be spent or how her husband should serve her. She might fear that he will abandon her just like her father left her mother. She might have a sense of entitlement: her husband owes her a big house, a nice car, and beautiful clothes. She might wrestle with idols that rule her heart, like perfectly behaved children or an out-of-this-world sex life with her husband. Expectations, fears, anger, entitlements, apathy, and idolatries are underlying dynamics that can define and rule any situation. Unless the pastor draws them out and makes them explicit, it is hard to deal with much in a person's life or situation. The love of the world takes many different forms, some of them brazen, others subtle. But a person is helped when she is alerted to what she is not sensible of, then directed to Christ as the true object of worship (see 1 John 1:8–10; 2:15–17; 3:1–3).

Show Consequences

Every decision in life—whether large or small—has consequences. This is the biblical principle of sowing and reaping. The type of seed you plant is the type of crop you carry home (Gal. 6:7–10). In pastoral counseling on the front end of decisions, it helps to explore the different alternatives a person might be facing and to trace out the logical consequences of certain choices or habits. Based on a pastor's experience and counsel of others, he will be able to describe likely outcomes of a decision. In fact, a pastor will find himself in situations where he needs to speak prophetically—not in the strict, direct-word-from-the-Lord sense, but rather in the sense of issuing a clear and sober warning of certain consequences. Such warnings should be accompanied by hope-filled descriptions of the blessings that come from submitting to God. Basically, you are challenging people to develop a vision of where their actions, attitudes, and desires will take them, for good or ill.

Confront and Reorient

Pastors often have hard conversations with hardened or foolish people. Confrontation is a normal part of pastoral life, and it is part of the solemn charge to proclaim the Word (2 Tim. 4:1–5). If a shepherd loves his sheep, he will warn and exhort them when they stray. A pastor who does not confront when he should is not being loving; he is being fearful. But God is with the one who seeks out wanderers, even when they don't know they're wandering (James 5:19–20).

Knowing how to confront in a specific situation is not always easy. But you should always speak from Scripture about what is being confronted, why it is displeasing to God, and how it shows up in a person's life. Confrontation should always be delivered with redemptive intent and personal commitment. Often the warning will go unheeded, and a person will step over the cliff into blatant sin. This is not necessarily a commentary on the quality of the confrontation. You hold up the warning sign, but only God's power can enable people to heed it.

Suggest Short-Term and Long-Term Goals

When a person is lost in the fog of difficulty, unable to see the step ahead, sometimes the best thing to do is to suggest some short-term and long-term goals. While change is mysterious and often incremental, this doesn't mean the counseling process is nebulous. We are called to specific action as we live out our faith (1 Pet. 1:13–19). Simple, practically oriented goals that address the problem can be remarkably helpful for getting someone out of a fog.

Setting goals will take some prep work on the pastor's part, since often people in the midst of trouble can't figure it out for themselves. Just keep one thing in mind: goals should only involve what a counselee is directly responsible for. We should not set goals that are dependent on other factors. So instead of setting a goal for a crummy husband to have a better marriage next week (which would be dependent upon his wife as well), you set a goal for him to confess his sin to her and ask for her forgiveness. Or instead of setting a goal for a depressed person to feel more hopeful in two weeks, you set a goal for things he can more directly control, like Bible intake, service to others, or exercise.

WRAPPING IT UP

Just like in the first session, we'll end by giving hope, assigning prep work, setting expectations for upcoming meetings, and praying for counselees. Sometimes it helps to get them to summarize what they got out of the meeting. Before you close in prayer, you may ask, "What one or two things did you get out of our time?" Don't be discouraged if what they saw or heard was not what you wanted them to understand. This summary moment provides yet another opportunity to remind people of the glories of Christ and God's perspective on the situation. So if they are missing something significant in their recounting of the session, take a moment to patiently instruct and encourage.

We'll round this chapter out with a few practical considerations. First, a word on pacing counseling well. Urgent problems will need more attention on the front end of the counseling process, usually weekly meetings. If a person calls threatening suicide, you'll drop everything else to address it right away. Problems that are not as urgent can be more spaced out. A church member who suffers from long-term chronic illness might need a once-a-month check-in to be encouraged and to keep a godly perspective. Pacing counseling appointments well comes with experience and knowledge of the folks you're serving.

If possible, give people enough time to study, pray, talk with friends, and work on things between sessions. Let them show that they are taking your conversations seriously and are willing to implement what they learned. Scheduling meetings too frequently may not leave adequate time to implement change.

Two ways the counseling task can become excessively burdensome on the pastor are when counseling takes up too much time and when it takes up too much effort. Regarding time, a pastor has to be careful that counseling does not crowd out preparation for preaching. Sometimes guilt drives this, sometimes fear. People need you, and you don't want to let them down. While what we said in the opening chapter is true—you do need to tend the sheep—you must not let the demands of personal ministry of the Word crowd out necessary labor in the public ministry of the Word. This takes wisdom, since there will be crisis weeks when you will have to step into the pulpit with five fewer hours of prep than you needed. But if you are consistently stepping into the pulpit without adequate preparation, this will be detrimental to your people in the long term. Don't be afraid to say no to individuals in order to say yes to the congregation.

Regarding effort, as you meet with people over the course of time, be careful not to do most of the work in counseling. Consider what we call the 80/20 rule. The person you're helping needs to be responsible to do 80 percent of the work in any given counseling session, with you guiding him or her with good questions, a few Scripture texts, and appropriate advice. Generally speaking, less mature believers will need more help from you in session, such as teaching or offering advice. And you should happily serve them in this way. But, as we said about a person who doesn't follow through on prep work, you will encounter folks who come to sessions only to mope about their problem and not to work at it. They consistently respond to questions with "I don't know" or "I don't care" or "I don't want to." In these situations, a straightforward conversation about who should be doing the heavy lifting is necessary. You'll learn the difference between folks who are genuinely hurting and unable to move and those who simply aren't willing to.

Questions to Keep in Mind but Not Necessarily Ask during a Counseling Session

- Is this person saved? Does he or she understand the gospel? If not, what can I do to help him or her grow in understanding the gospel? If this person is not a Christian, how does that adjust my counsel?

- What are the shapes and contours of this individual's faith? What does faithfulness look like in his or her circumstances?

- Where do I see suffering in this person's life? Does he or she have a biblical view of suffering, or is it skewed by the world?

- Where do I see sin in this man's life? Does he see it, or is he blind to this sin?

- Where has this woman been sinned against? Is reconciliation possible? How can I help her see the pathway to reconciliation?

- Are there any signs of hope in this situation? What are the evidences of God's grace in this person's life?

SIX

The Final Meeting

Finishing is often the hardest part of a construction job, and not because the tasks are more difficult. It's hard because after so much effort exerted consulting blueprints, laying a foundation, and framing the house, a worker has to stay motivated to do the small steps necessary to make the finished structure look good. Anyone who's had to do finish trim and a final coat of paint after weeks of construction knows this. Finishing well takes effort and thought, even for a pastor who has already given so much. The majority of the labor is behind you. Just a bit more will help ensure that what was accomplished stays accomplished.

So as we consider the final meeting, we will lay out two elements that make for a settled conclusion of counseling and transition into the regular care of the church: (1) review the main themes of the counseling, and (2) plan for regular care. But before we unpack the two simple steps of the final session, let's consider some basic indicators that the counseling process has run its course. How does a counselor know when to conclude?

WHEN TO END

The decision to bring the counseling process to a close is sometimes clear, but often not. You will probably be aware, with some uneasiness, that not every problem has been solved. You will sense the need for more growth or the person's desire that counseling continue regularly. But these are not adequate reasons to perpetuate counseling. When to end counseling is always a judgment call that requires wisdom. It's best to frame the decision with some clear criteria. We will start with positive indicators of when to conclude counseling, then move to some less pleasant ones.

Positive Signs

The counselees understand their problem and are equipped to handle it. The best indicator for ending counseling is that the individuals have been adequately equipped to respond in faith to their troubles and are showing a consistent pattern of doing so. Perhaps a benefit of this is also that the symptoms have lightened: the initial depression isn't so bad; the husband and wife have reconciled and have rebuilt their trust; the young man hooked on pornography has had a considerable reprieve from his sexual sin. The pressure of the original problem is no longer wreaking havoc on life. So they don't feel the need to meet with you anymore. And as much as you love them, you don't feel the need to meet with them either.

In the course of your care for them, another person's care emerges as more effective. If you are counseling in the context of the local church, you will be utilizing other couples or individuals to come alongside a counselee. Often these other individuals become more effective than you in addressing the issues of this person's heart. This is not a threat to your position as pastor, but rather a mark of the church working well. It should thrill you that others demonstrate a skill or have an insight that you didn't. If you recognize this as the case, it may be best to transition counselees to the care of others. Just be sure to maintain pastoral oversight of that care.

Negative Signs

Sadly, not all counseling ends with a positive conclusion. Sometimes other reasons compel a transition to other counselors or other types of care.

Things don't seem to be changing at all. You have tried to help people for a while, and things just don't seem to be going anywhere. They have apparently been striving to make changes, but the problem they started with is still plaguing them. Maybe it's even gotten worse. This may be from a lack of insight or skill on your part, or it may be from hard-heartedness, ignorance, or other factors on their part. Usually it's a bit of both. But the point is, nothing seems to be making a difference. That's a good time to consider making a shift to someone who might be able to do more than you. We'll talk more about this in the last chapter.

They aren't interested in working. You will be in counseling situations when counselees will basically use meeting time to gripe, gossip, and complain. But when it comes to the hard work of studying Scripture, thinking through heart motives, confronting sin, or facing their own misgivings, they just don't want to do it. These folks expect you to do the heavy lifting in the sessions. But we don't serve our people by indulging their sense of "doing something" about the problem by coming to counseling when they refuse to actually *do something*. Do not let people deceive themselves into thinking they're putting forth effort when they're not. If they do not do the prep work and are uninterested in answering the questions you lay out, then for their own good the counseling needs to end. To let people think they are helping themselves by showing up for appointments when, in fact, their hearts remain unteachable is to let them engage in a kind of self-deceit.

They don't trust you. There will also be situations where your mistakes are painfully evident. Maybe you messed up by speaking into a matter without understanding it or by responding to them in plain frustration. You've forgotten appointments or been unable to fit them into your schedule with reasonable turnover. The point is, they have lost trust in you—whether through your fault or their unrealistic expectations. Regardless, people will not follow your guidance if they don't trust you, which means it's time to end counseling. If they are unwilling to trust counsel from anyone else in the church, it may also be time for them to consider moving on to another church.

They need more help than you can offer. Their problem is intense enough to need more time or expertise than you have to offer. You wish you had more time to spend with them, but fulfilling your other responsibilities would become impossible since your counselees would need more than just a one-hour-a-week conversation. For instance, eating disorders can become so out of control that strugglers need daily conversations. Or maybe you wish you had more skill to know the contours of a particular problem. But you don't have the insight, skill, or time needed to sort through the complexity.

Now, part of the purpose of this primer is to convince you that the threshold of what you can handle is higher than you might realize. But we also want to recognize that certain troubles have become so spiritually complex or physiologically engrained that you should seek someone with greater skill. The goal is not to pass people off; rather, it's to get them the help they need.

Don't feel like a failure if you have to refer them to someone else in the church (another pastor or another mature believer) or someone outside the church (a professional counselor or doctor in your community). Sometimes the best way to shepherd individuals is not to continue the work yourself, but to point them in the right direction—to someone who can give them the time and attention they need. Again, we'll say more on referral in the last chapter.

Regardless of which one of these applies to your situation, each of them is a good indicator that you should end counseling by suggesting a final meeting. Some folks will be more than happy that counseling is over. Others will be alarmed. For the latter, a final meeting is a killer for them. They want counseling to go on much longer than is needed, perhaps even arguing with you about how they need more help. If you, in wisdom (not impatience), have concluded that things should wind down, then be gracious and stay the course in bringing things to a conclusion. Don't let the pitfalls and pressures of overly needy people set the pace of your counseling. Humbly listen to their concerns; pray about the matter; and then you determine what is best.

Demonstrating Humility and Courage in the Face of Failure

Even when things go poorly in counseling, it can be a good opportunity to take stock of why things didn't work out. First, as a pastor, be humble enough to hear godly criticism. Did you put too much pressure on the husband to change, only to find out the wife was keeping secrets from you? Was your application of Scripture superficial? Were you impatient with them? Were you prone to frustration with them?

As their pastor, you must also be courageous enough to have hard conversations about why things didn't work out. Were the counselees so prideful or so quick to blame others that nothing was going to change until they were willing to repent and take ownership of the problem? Did you give godly advice they spurned? Were they giving way to fear, or being reckless in their treatment of others, or giving themselves over to worldliness? Sometimes you'll be the only person willing to say the hard things needed to make a difference in their lives—and the only one who will do so with a graciousness that shows them that your ultimate motive is love.

ELEMENTS OF THE FINAL SESSION

The two parts of the final session include, first, reviewing the major themes about what God has done through the whole process of counseling; second, entrusting the person to the regular ministries and care of the church.

We should mention here that both you and the counselee should be aware before your final meeting that your next meeting will be your last. If you spring it on people during the meeting, they tend to get panicky. Communicating with them prior to the meeting will convey that this is a measured decision, considered carefully in the context of a plan.

Review the Main Themes of Counseling

Like the final paragraph of many a well-written essay, the final counseling session should summarize the main themes of your counseling. There is a positive function and a negative function to this summary—more specifically, commendation and warning.

Commendation. Positively, you commend and even celebrate the Lord's work in people's lives. Emphasize the positive changes in their *responses* to trouble more than any positive changes in the trouble itself. This helps keep the emphasis on their walking by faith amid changing circumstances. You are taking stock of what God has done in someone's heart. This involves both commending the counselee for new and faithful responses and recognizing those responses as God's work in them (Phil. 2:12–13).

To do this, ask questions to encourage the person to reflect on his or her life:

- What has God taught you?
- Where were you when we began this process?
- How did you see your responses to trouble change over the course of counseling?
- Where did hope enter in?
- When were you the most discouraged?
- Do you trust God more now than you did at the start?
- What lessons did you learn from God's Word?
- What do you understand about yourself, God's character, redemption, or your own sanctification that you didn't understand before?

You are asking these things not to feel good about your pastoral guidance, but rather to boast about the kindness of God during the person's season of struggle. You are giving thanks to God, which is a vital part of change (Col. 3:15–17).

In the attempt to survive, people tend to lose the perspective of the whole because of their preoccupation with immediate feelings or situations. Most of the time, people tend to focus on their shortcomings and failures more than on their obedience. Even if faith is often small and flickering, as a pastor you fan it into flame through thankful commendation of God's presence in their lives. You are calling people to look up from their immediate concerns and scan the broad horizon of all that God has done.

But maybe there's not all that much to positively commend. Maybe this is your final session because of one of the unpleasant reasons we listed earlier. In these cases, use this time to speak of God's long-term plan of change for those who are truly his. That this season did not produce a harvest does not mean nothing was accomplished. Perhaps this was the time for planting new biblical insights or watering old ones; the harvest is yet to come. You can always commend the Lord's dedication to complete any work he begins (Phil. 1:6).

Warning. Seldom is everything resolved by the end of counseling. Even positive changes from counseling are often in their infancy and will have to mature over time. Life is not tidy. Sin and suffering have consequences that endure long into the future (Gal. 6:7–8). People will need to maintain vigilance over their souls. As a pastor, your job is to equip them to do so. Thus we have the second function of reviewing the main themes of counseling: to warn people of pitfalls.

In the course of counseling, you have helped them think through the different dynamics of sin and suffering that have plagued their lives. Set these again on the table, review the pertinent biblical promises and commands, and remind them of the plan of action. For instance, a young man is fighting against porn use, so you ask what he would do if his accountability relationships fizzle out or the guilt and shame of failing again press in. Talk to him about what he should do if he wants to pursue marriage with a certain young lady. Or consider the grieving widow who has spent many months with you working slowly and deliberately through her sorrow. The dark clouds have lifted, and she is again engaging with others and relishing her time in the Word. You'll want to help her think through what to do when those sad moments return, how she can relate to her adult children moving forward, and what to do if she finds herself desiring again to be married.

In these examples, you are attempting to shore up the biblical principles and practical tactics for handling future situations that may tempt people to fall back into old patterns of response. These warnings should be hope-filled but sober, as the writer of Hebrews demonstrates so well. In chapter 6, after giving what may be the most frightful warning in all of Scripture, he continues, "Though we speak in this way, yet in your case, beloved, we feel sure of better things—things that belong to salvation" (v. 9), then he goes on to commend the evidences of grace in these believers' lives. As a pastor, you are simply mimicking the biblical author's approach: sober warning in the context of warm commendation.

Plan for Regular Care

Now that you've reviewed the main themes in a way that commends positive change and warns of falling back into old patterns, lay out a simple plan for what it means for counselees to return to the regular means of care in the church body. As the counseling process ends, pastors no longer sit on the front lines of the problems addressed, but entrust people to be sustained through the regular means of grace that God provides for his children. Here we should think about the public, personal, and private ministries of the Word.

Public ministries of the Word. Never let counselees overlook the power of the Word of God preached and taught. This means making the public ministries of the Word an explicit part of their ongoing care. Don't assume this; remind counselees of the power of receiving and meditating on the Word delivered by the pastors of their church. If someone who wants to grow in grace does not prioritize the public gathering of believers, her growth will be stunted (Heb. 10:23–25). As a pastor, you can have more confidence to end counseling when you know some-one's soul will be nourished weekly as she continues to sit under the public teaching of God's Word at church.

Personal ministries of the Word. Consider the means of fellowship and mutual care in your church, and make the best use of them. You can think of formal and informal personal ministry. Formal ministry would include a community group, where regular meetings around the Word take place for the purpose of accountability and encouragement. Help counselees know the role their community groups should play in their ongoing care.

Informal ministry may be a strong friendship in the church. From the very first session, the pastor should ask about the counselee's relationships within the congregation. During counseling, the goal is to make sure the person grows more connected to the church body so that when counseling is done, the pastor can have confidence that others in the church will continue to invest in the person's life. Loving redemptive relationships are vital for Christian growth and can serve as a safety net when things are going poorly.

Friends or small-group members will want to consult with the pastor about what to do if significant troubles arise again.

The best plan is simply to have them tell you if there is ongoing failure or resistance on the part of the counselee. This will require direct pastoral involvement. But for the regular ups and downs of life, the care of the body is more effective than we often realize.

Private ministries of the Word. As counseling draws to a close, the pastor should consider what final prep work he can give the counselee. The goal is to help the person to consistently seek Christ in private devotions so that the Word has yet another opportunity to do its work (Isa. 55:10–11).

You should think in terms of both Scripture and other resources. Regarding Scripture, perhaps the counselee would benefit from a list of biblical texts to work through in the weeks and months ahead. You could also provide him with basic questions to be asking of the text and of himself that will help keep his Bible reading appropriately focused. Regarding other resources, there may be a good book or article he can read as a way to continue thinking about how biblical principles apply to his struggles.

Keep in mind that in recommending both Scripture reading plans and other resources, you don't need to limit your focus to the themes you covered in counseling. Christians always benefit by growing in the knowledge of God and his character. The point is to help people know God from his Word. This is always the best long-term plan for Christian discipleship.

If counselees have dealt with serious suicidal thoughts or other manifestations of extreme mental distress in the past, remind them to seek immediate help if they experience them again. Compel them also to call you or a designated individual from church so that the church can care for them in whatever season of difficulty they may go through.

Once you have laid out the plan of regular care, make sure you pray. Don't let things finish without taking them before the throne and reminding them of the hope they have in Christ. Use this final prayer to recap the things covered in this last session and throughout your entire time. This closing prayer will again help them see both how the Lord's grace is much greater than their problems and how he is specifically working in their lives.

CONCLUDING THOUGHTS

Always leave the door open at the end. This is not necessarily a promise of more counseling but rather of dedication to see them continue to grow through whatever means the Lord would use. Be clear about your expectations for the future, especially about your role after counseling is done. Do not become inaccessible to them. You should welcome a casual conversation after church or an occasional phone call as part of your ongoing care. Often these conversations are the little lifelines that help people stay the course.

And every so often, you might find them to be a lifeline for you. God can use these conversations to remind you that he's at work even when you're not.

Part Three

CONTEXT

SEVEN

Never Laboring Alone: Toward a Culture of Discipleship

Well, there it is. The process of laboring through a problem with someone is complete. But what is not complete is our view of the broader setting of that care. If the pastor's counseling were all there is to the change process, you should prepare to give up the habit of sleeping each night. If you labor as though the spiritual well-being of every member directly depends on you, you will eventually fold under such an impossible burden. God in his wisdom assigned the task of discipleship not to a single man, nor even to a team of men, but to the entire church.

In these final two chapters, we want to look at how the church and the resources in your community can help people through the troubles of life. In this chapter, we are moving from street view to city view, from the pastoral counseling room to the church as a whole. In the next, we will notice that the city view also shows the surrounding landscape; the church is located in a community with counselors, doctors, and other parachurch resources. So in this chapter, we will emphasize the importance of never laboring alone, but building a culture of discipleship in your congregation. And in the next, we will offer guidance for wisely making use of outside medical, professional, and parachurch resources.

A CULTURE OF DISCIPLESHIP

Defining a culture is a tricky task, but if you've ever experienced what is described as culture shock, you have a good reference point for understanding what a culture actually is. When a city boy moves to the country, he may experience a depressive boredom from seeing only a handful of people in this new setting of quiet, stretching farmland. His expectations of the world as bustling with people and noise are unmet. He is out of his culture.

A culture is a set of shared beliefs, values, and practices. Just as every community has one, so does every congregation. We share collective expectations, and each member of a community contributes to them. Thus, every member of your church is a culture maker. Everything members say or do, the things they value, the money they spend, the ways they show love or work through discontent, their practical life choices at school or work—all these things shape the culture of your church.

But as the pastor, you are the primary shaper of the church's culture. Because you preach most frequently, your beliefs and values are far more influential in steering the culture of the church. What matters to you usually defines what matters to the church. This influence is a grave privilege (Heb. 13:7).

So, as pastors, we are compelled to ask ourselves what really matters most to us. Why are we in ministry in the first place?

We know the ultimate answer is to bring glory to God, but by what means? Eloquent sermons? Growing public influence? A stable and expanding congregation? These can be acceptable *means*, but they are insufficient *values*. The way to glorify God is to make disciples. This task should be in the deepest part of a pastor's value system. And he should radiate this as a value his people should share.

So, what do you expect from your members? Is discipling a normal expectation in your congregation, a life-or-death priority? Scripture makes it clear that making disciples is a task of pastors as well as church members. The night before his death, Jesus told his disciples what should characterize this new covenant community he was establishing: "A new commandment I give to you, that you love one another: just as I have loved you, you also are to love one another. By this all people will know that you are my disciples, if you have love for one another" (John 13:34–35). Christ commanded the members of the new covenant community to share with one another the love that he had shared with each one of them.

Paul picks up on this central command and applies it to church life: love, spoken and performed, is how each member builds up the whole. "Speaking the truth in love, we are to grow up in every way into him who is the head, into Christ, from whom the whole body, joined and held together by every joint with which it is equipped, when each part is working properly, makes the body grow so that it builds itself up in love" (Eph. 4:15–16). To be built up in Christ means to be formed as a disciple.

Thus, discipleship requires members to labor for each other in love. Every Christian is obliged to love others in God's scheme of discipleship—which includes practical labors like being devoted to each other (Rom. 12:10), honoring and accepting one another (15:7), instructing others (15:14), being compassionate and quick to forgive (Eph. 4:32), and lending courage (1 Thess. 5:11). This is hard labor. Gloriously hard.

Even though it's hard, or perhaps *especially* because it's hard, a pastor cannot be shy about the New Testament's vision of discipleship involving the active participation of all members. It offends common consumerist expectations about church: "I give money to the church, and the church gives me what I want—and only what I want. What I want is good teaching to help me with my life and a pastor to help me with my troubles."

Perhaps even more offensive than treading on people's expectations about church is stepping on their deeply held assumptions about relationships in general: "My business is my business, and yours is yours." But if you search Scripture for the doctrine of personal privacy, you won't find much material to construct it. This is unnerving to people. So creating a culture that counters this mind-set takes patience and skill.

Please understand, you are *not* asking your people to live without proprietary boundaries, as if everyone in the church has a right to everyone else's personal business. Living in a fallen world requires us to wear clothes. We rightly entrust personal things only to trustworthy people. Our point is, rather, that you should be building trustworthy people who are both willing and equipped to help others when trouble comes.

We should strive to make church a place where being anonymous or nominal is difficult to pull off. We want the healthy pressure of the preached Word and Christian relationships to press in on the believer's life. In other words, your people should know that active discipleship is an expectation of your church. So ask yourself on a regular basis, am I leading my church in

Christlike character—love, service, hope, self-sacrifice—so that discipling one another is normal and expected?

KEY EXPECTATIONS TO EMPHASIZE

We would like to offer some suggestions for answering this question well. Our advice will not be primarily organizational, though we will give some practical tips. Creating a culture of discipleship is not first about creating programs, classes, groups, or other kinds of structural fixes within the church's life. Certainly, mentoring programs may connect older and wiser Christians with younger and less mature ones. Small groups may build more intimate relationships with other believers. Age-graded Sunday school classes may offer specific instruction for various life situations. Support groups may care for members in certain life stages (newly married, new parents) or struggles (divorce, depression). All of these can be helpful structures. But a culture of discipleship can thrive without them.

We aren't saying this because such structural realities are unhelpful—both of our churches offer almost all of these structures. But if we ever find them failing to assist discipleship, we are willing to jettison them. Discipleship, as we've established, means to love one another by speaking and living according to God's Word together.

A culture of discipleship means that members don't have to sign up for anything or get permission to love one another. It is a church culture where it is normal for the members to take initiative to love one another and do each other spiritual good. This church culture is not a program, but something that flows in the lifeblood of the church. As the pastor, you cannot *make* members actively pursue one another in love, but you can set expectations that will promote it. Here are three expectations you should regularly set before your congregation to promote a discipleship culture.

Membership

This first expectation may seem odd to many pastors, but membership turns out to be one of the most important expectations of discipleship. Church membership is less like belonging to a social group or local gym or book club, and more like a marriage. Marriage is a covenant commitment. A husband and wife commit themselves to each other, and the overflow of that commitment is a lifelong relationship of love and self-sacrifice. Church membership is similar. In the church, a group of believers regularly gathers together because of their commitment to God and to one another.

When a believer joins the church, he gets much more than a membership card. He receives the commitment of other believers to his spiritual good, and he commits to theirs. A person joining your church should not expect to be comfortable as a Sunday-only member. He is signing away his individualism. Membership means commitment to the church as a whole. Such a commitment is foundational to disciple making. Meaningful membership makes a difference.

As people join your church, make clear to them the connection between membership and discipleship. Explain your disciple-making expectation to prospective new members. In your membership class, tell folks that discipleship is a part of what it means to be a part of your church. Ask them personally, "Are you willing both to be discipled and to disciple others?"

You also want to make clear to your people the connection between membership and *discipline*. This word typically evokes unpleasant feelings—and rightfully so, since even Scripture acknowledges that it is necessarily unpleasant (Heb. 12:11) in order to bring about its happy purpose: "the peaceful fruit of righteousness." Church discipline is simply the members of a church loving one another by confronting patterns of sin that destroy the soul and defile the church (Matt. 18:15–20; 1 Cor. 5:1–5). Like all real love, it hates what is evil and loves what is good by handling one another with both patience and honesty about sin (Rom. 12:9–21). Church discipline is about more than its final expression of excommunication; it is part of the regular vigilance members have over one another's souls.

Counseling can be part of this regular vigilance. Members who seek counseling should understand from the beginning that as a ministry of discipleship, counseling is part of a broader accountability to the church. Counseling is therefore a safe place for those struggling against sin, even if they fall often in that struggle. But counseling is not a safe place for those who willfully continue patterns of clear and unrepentant sin. The line between genuine struggle and unrepentance is not always clear. (Thank God for the shared wisdom of an elder board or pastoral staff.) Because we don't have the immediate insight of the Holy Spirit, patient, hope-filled accountability with clear and reasonable standards is the best way to test the long-term trajectory of someone on the line. Our point on discipline is simply that church accountability does not get checked at the door of the counseling room, and this is for the good of the counselee and the church at large.

In pastoral counseling, the threat of church discipline should quietly sit in the back of the counselee's mind, acting as a deterrent to unrepentant sin. It's a sad and sobering day when a church member is excommunicated from the church, but we understand church discipline to be a vital step of accountability for a person's soul.

Equipping

Second, your people should expect to be equipped *by you* for the task of disciple making. You equip your people in two primary ways: by teaching and by modeling.

Pastors must teach discipleship as Christ's beautiful design for the benefit of his church. Only as members see this beauty for themselves in the pages of Scripture will they find the godly motivation to obey. Pastors can motivate their people to do disciplish things by making them feel guilty or appealing to their pride. Such motivation is not worthy of Christ's bride. To get people to act on the Bible's instruction, they must believe it. And to believe it, they must be instructed by it, again and again.

We are not implying that every public teaching is on the topic of disciple making. Rather, we want you to think of it as a thread that weaves its way throughout your teaching ministry, as it does throughout the New Testament's instruction to the church. Regularly teach disciple-making expectations for *all* of your current members. This can be done during your Sunday sermons, in a Sunday school series, or in an occasional training seminar on discipling. Pastors, as you teach, make this theme practical for your congregation. For example:

- "We want our members to have enough confidence in the gospel to live transparently. We should not be uncomfortable asking hard questions or threatened by being asked them";
- or, "Let's pray that our vision of a fruitful life will be shaped more by what Scripture says about the church and less by what culture says about personal success";

- or, "What person in this congregation might benefit from some sacrifice of your time and attention?"

Instruct members in the priority of Christian discipleship, so that they can grow in their own personal conviction of what Scripture teaches on this subject.

Pastors must also model discipleship. If you expect your church members to make discipling a priority, you need to set an example. This means you should be personally discipling men in your congregation to live as godly husbands, fathers, and workers. And these men should know that they are expected to do the same. Pastors' wives and other godly woman should be doing the same.

In addition to personally modeling discipling, perhaps even better, pastors should *display* models of discipling. In your teaching, find ways to tell the congregation about encouraging examples of discipling, like Matt's investment in Ryan. Matt, the electrician, started meeting with Ryan, the college student, every other Tuesday morning. Ryan would come to Matt's house for Bible study, prayer, and a stiff cup of coffee. Because Ryan was a new believer, he still didn't really get what the Christian life should look like. Because Matt had never discipled someone before, he felt uneasy about how he was conducting the Bible study with Ryan.

But one moment captured the power of discipleship. Matt was about to start the study when his daughters started acting up. Matt excused himself to talk with his daughters in the next room. When Matt returned, Ryan said something that surprised him: "I don't know what we're going to study today, but what I just learned by watching you instruct your daughters was invaluable." Ryan grew up in a destructive home where his father screamed at him all of his life. Gracious instruction was something he had never seen before. As Ryan watched Matt's regular life as a Christian, he got a snapshot of biblical parenting. Discipling should be taught, but it must also be *caught* as people see Christianity in action.

As people see discipleship in action, they must then be challenged to live it out. After several years of pouring into Ryan, Matt encouraged him to find someone to disciple. Out of the investment made in him, Ryan should invest in others. Jesus started with twelve. Just as those twelve went out and made more disciples, and those folks in turn made more disciples, so also we should be disciple-making Christians. They set an example for us to follow.

As you teach about discipling and give examples in your sermon application, you should avoid glorifying individuals or focusing only on success stories. Your people should hear that apparent failure will always be part of this labor, and the Lord is honored in it all.

In addition to the teaching and modeling, pastors can publicly encourage discipleship in a number of other ways: commend and give out good books on discipling; have designated times for testimonies of discipleship; and regularly pray about the discipleship relationships going on in the church.

Connecting

A third expectation to communicate is that people will connect with each other. Actually getting together with another person is necessary for discipleship to occur. But before anyone starts typing up a spreadsheet, let us explain what we mean. The ideal is that discipleship relationships come as the result of members initiating with one another. A church member has committed to the body, been equipped with some idea of how to disciple, and reaches out to another member in the congregation. If members are prayerfully watching over each other, God will guide them to those relationships.

The pastor will have to remind folks often of this step in the process—of actually reaching out to connect. It's not enough for you to lay theological foundations; you have to call on people to actively build on them. Some church folk are natural initiators; others are more reticent in their disposition. Offer encouragement pertinent to both.

Not all connecting will be member initiated, though. Using their personal knowledge of the church, pastors should regularly connect those with needs with others who can meet them. If someone is struggling with finances, is there anyone in the church particularly gifted in money management? If a couple is grieving the death of a child, is there a couple who has already navigated those dark waters? If a man is fighting against pornography, what other man in the congregation is characterized by sexual purity? Basically, you are connecting people who need wisdom with those who know where to find it in God's Word.

If pastors have invested in a culture of discipleship, then approaching someone to help a struggling member will not seem an imposition. The pastor should help lay out a plan of action, a time frame, and how pastoral oversight will be maintained. This will give members greater confidence in helping the struggling Christian. But then it's up to the members to take it from there.

SO WHAT DOES THIS HAVE TO DO WITH COUNSELING?

You might be checking the front cover to see the title again. *The Pastor and Counseling*? How does all this talk about a culture of discipleship relate?

If you asked an average member at your church to disciple another believer, our guess is that he or she could eventually figure out how to read the Bible with him, pray together, and share honestly about both their lives. But if you asked this same average member to talk with someone who is suicidal, to help an adulterer overcome her shame, or to sort through the obsessive thought patterns of someone with an eating disorder, his or her confidence level would probably drop significantly.

When a typical Christian hears about the hard, confusing stuff in the Christian life, he or she will probably back away. Most Christians assume that the really messy stuff needs to be handled solely by the professionals—pastors or counselors. Certainly more-experienced folks may need to help someone with particularly difficult troubles. But this does not mean that a typical Christian is helpless.

Every Christian is capable of helping, even with the really hard stuff in the Christian life. With the sword of the Spirit (Eph. 6:17), Christ's love in their hearts (Gal. 5:6), and a willingness to serve (Mark 10:43–45), nothing can stop them from doing some effective good. God uses his Word to offer wisdom for responding rightly to any circumstance under the sun. That wisdom is available for all who seek it, and Christians can do this together formally or informally.

Seeking wisdom in a discipleship setting is really not different from seeking wisdom in a counseling setting. It follows the general pattern we have laid out already. Seeking God's wisdom involves listening with a discerning ear, considering heart responses, and speaking the truth of Scripture in love. Counseling simply involves more intensive exploration, more formal structure, and problem-specific expertise.

Basically, pastor, if you want help with your counseling,

start by building a culture of discipleship in your church. If you are building a people committed to one another's spiritual good, they will be more interested in counseling as a tool that can help toward that end. As more of your members become interested in discipling, you can also start equipping them to be competent to counsel by the Word, applying it to some of life's messier problems.

If you don't want to do counseling by yourself for the next ten years, start praying about building a counseling ministry in your church. Think about how to equip members to face hard things. Read about how to build a lay counseling ministry. Ask other pastors who have already done this in their churches.

Deliberately investing in and training church members can help dispel fears and build confidence. A combination of public teaching and private small-group instruction can instill basic counseling concepts. You might think, "I barely have time to counsel; how am I supposed to write and teach others?" Fortunately for all of us, both self-published curriculums (such as John Henderson's *Equipped to Counsel: A Training Course in Biblical Counseling*) and more formal curriculums (such as CCEF's small-group materials, including Timothy S. Lane and Paul David Tripp's *How People Change* and Tripp's *Instruments in the Redeemer's Hands*) have hit the market over the last few years. Most are very easy to use and understand. If you have a few mature Christians in your congregation, take them through a biblical counseling curriculum with the express goal of having them teach it to others.

But don't just train your members in counseling. One of the best ways to help your congregation to understand how to handle difficult problems is by modeling counseling *in front of* them. For example, if you are counseling John, ask his small-group leader or a trusted friend (with John's permission) to join your counseling sessions; by doing so, you equip others for discipleship as you build into John. They will hear what questions you ask, observe your disposition and active listening skills, and get firsthand exposure to John's issues. At the end of a session, you can discuss with these friends how to help John throughout the rest of the week.

Pastor, don't do counseling by yourself. Asking family, friends, or fellow church members to join counseling sessions is an easy way to start equipping others. Make it a priority to invite others into the counseling room. If a member is uncomfortable sharing his business with others, this is a discipleship opportunity. Teach him the humility to seek help and the need for others to help him discern his heart (Heb. 3:12–13). Help him to think through who may already know enough about the issues to join the counseling sessions. If there is no one, then what key people—other church leaders or mature Christians in the congregation—could be trusted? This has the benefit of both helping the counselee and training others in counseling.

We should note that if a counselee remains hesitant, a pastor should not compel him to have someone present. He may not be ready, and that's okay.

NEVER LABOR ALONE

Pastor, if you are stuck in the trenches, overwhelmed with your church members' counseling problems, and not sure how to find relief, a culture of discipleship can go a long way in helping.

As you build this culture of discipleship, keep in mind that a church's culture does not change overnight. You'll have to take a long-term view. Change is always gradual and never universal. You will have pockets of the congregation who get it and want more of it, and others who are less inclined toward it. Don't be too encouraged by those who get it, and don't be too discouraged by those who do not. Set simple goals of laying out the disciple-making expectations described above, then move on to some of the next steps in equipping people for a counseling ministry. Your focus should be on whatever reasonable steps you can take now, and then on whatever possible steps will come next.

If you feel like the burdens of counseling are too great for you, those feelings are accurate. But do not be discouraged; be dependent. Specifically, depend on what God has determined to give his New Testament people—the whole church speaking the truth in love. Don't labor alone. Reach out to other mature believers as a good place to start.

In the end, we can only labor in the strength that God supplies. Why? In order that in everything God may be glorified through Jesus Christ. His glory is what we strive for. The apostle Peter, the one whom Jesus told to tend his lambs those three painful times, reminds us of this. In fact, his words to us are a great summary of the culture of discipleship we are striving for.

> Above all, keep loving one another earnestly, since love covers a multitude of sins. Show hospitality to one another without grumbling. As each has received a gift, use it to serve one another, as good stewards of God's varied grace: whoever speaks, as one who speaks oracles of God; whoever serves, as one who serves by the strength that God supplies—in order that in everything God may be glorified through Jesus Christ. To him belong glory and dominion forever and ever. Amen. (1 Pet. 4:8–11)

EIGHT

Laboring Wisely: Using Outside Resources Well

In the previous chapter, our view zoomed out from the individual counseling process to the larger context of the church as a whole. We thought about how to develop a culture of discipleship in your congregation and how to raise up others to labor alongside you. In this chapter, we will zoom out a bit further to consider how to wisely use resources outside the church. Of the resources available, many will be very helpful and some less so, but even the helpful ones will need to be handled with wisdom.

We have done our best to argue that counseling is an important part of the pastor's labor for his people. When Jesus called you to shepherd his people, he called you to walk with them through complex and sometimes ugly problems. But we also know that pastors have limitations, both in time and in experience with the complexities of human trouble. Here are some indicators it may be time to seek outside help.

You're on your own and maxed out. You are pastoring an unhealthy church. Your congregation is not serious about discipleship. So when problems arise, you are basically on your own. Apart from your wife praying for you, there is really no one else who is willing to lend a hand.

You've tried your best without much effect. You have helped someone for months with a deeply ingrained problem. While there has been some progress, the trouble remains largely untouched. You've sacrificed much time and remain dedicated to the person, but you've reached the limits of your insight to help with patterns that are not changing.

You sense the need for further medical help. While you should have counselees seek regular medical advice from the beginning, sometimes people display bizarre behavior, intrusive thought patterns, or extreme emotional responses that seem uncontrollable. These may be indicators that their physiology needs further attention from a doctor.

You must disclose information that protects people from abuse or deadly harm. When a person threatens suicide, homicide, or any abuse of children, elderly folks, or dependent persons, you must immediately report to authorities. If you have reasonable suspicion or direct admission from your counselee that such abuse has occurred already, you must report this as well. Get to know your state's laws as well as whatever child-protective services it offers. The folks you see for counseling should know that you are required to disclose such things when they first start the process with you. Reporting to authorities does not mean you are being an untrustworthy pastor, and you can explain this with two simple facts: First, you are not permitted by law to determine guilt or innocence on your own authority.

Second, you will remain committed to shepherding their spiritual needs through whatever may come.

Pastoral ministry will bring all these types of situations your way. You can be ready now if you figure out *when* and *for what reasons* you will seek help in your local community. In this chapter we'll present some simple criteria that can be applied to whatever community your church is in.

The counseling resources you will find in your community will generally fall into one of three categories: (1) church or parachurch counseling, (2) professional counseling, (3) medical or psychiatric help. Each of these can be found in regular or residential forms. Regular care occurs as a series of appointments with a counselor or doctor. Residential treatment is more intensive and involves living away from home under the direction of counselors or doctors.

REFERRING TO OUTSIDE RESOURCES

As we discuss referral, we want to be careful with what we mean by it. By "referral," we are not implying that you are moving someone out of your care and into someone else's. You are this person's pastor and are called to watch over his or her soul. You maintain spiritual oversight of your members by helping them think through whatever counsel they receive from these other resources. As their shepherd, your primary goal is to keep Jesus Christ central to their understanding of genuine heart change.

Just to be clear: we are not saying that pastors oversee the outside resources directly. They function outside your authority in terms of their own practices and procedures. Rather, you are helping your people sort through the guidance they're receiving, making sure they critique it from a biblical standpoint.

This will help them determine for themselves if they want to continue with it or not.

Church or Parachurch Counseling

The place to start in your search for solid, local biblical counseling is to seek out other gospel-preaching, Bible-based churches in your area. You may find that they either offer counseling services as part of their ministry or have done their homework and found a reliable counselor in your area. So start by contacting a few like-minded churches in your community, and ask them who they use for counseling. Start your own referral list by using some of their recommended counselors.

If no other solid church in your area has done the research, you'll need to do your own. It probably won't be easy to find a counselor who fits with both your theology and your philosophy of care. But here are some helpful criteria.

First and foremost, you want to find a Christian who knows God's Word and knows how to relate its power to the problems of life. Is Scripture a regular and authoritative source of this person's counsel? You've probably experienced talking with a member whose counselor addressed how the problem expressed itself, but offered advice and strategies only marginally related to the Bible. If a counselor knows and trusts the Bible, you will know it in how he or she advises your member.

Second, you want someone who has a loving, gracious, trustworthy demeanor. Tone matters. Yes, a person will sometimes need a firm, loving rebuke. But that is best done after the counselor has earned the counselee's trust. A necessary step to earning trust is being a gracious person who approaches troubled people with the patient kindness of Jesus. On the whole, a counselor needs to be someone who is approachable and has a merciful disposition toward life's problems. Do not entrust your people to someone whose demeanor does not match what the Bible commands (1 Pet. 3:8), even if he ostensibly knows the Bible well.

Third, you need someone who can patiently persist through the complexity of life's problems. Patience is always a virtue, but especially in counseling because change is slow. Generally, problems get better in small steps, not large leaps. Proper expectations and a willingness to work within God's timing are important characteristics in a counselor who may help a struggler for months or even years.

Finally, you want someone who has the competence to handle the problem. Having no counselor is better than sending your member to a bad one. An incompetent counselor can quickly make things worse by holding a person to unrealistic expectations or by indulging self-oriented perspectives. A guy with a Bible is not enough. He has to have the quality of situational wisdom—the ability to recognize the fine nuances of human responses and understand how biblical truth shapes them. You don't necessarily need a counselor who specializes in a particular problem, as long as he has the tools to handle complexity in human life.

Even if you find someone who exemplifies these qualities, please remember that the counselor is simply helping a person through the specifics of an issue. You still need to stay in touch with your member to ensure that counsel is consistent with the Bible's promises of grace and expectations for godly living. Here are a few practical ways to stay engaged with counseling:

- Take some time to visit the counseling sessions. One of the best ways for you to learn how to deal with the problems that you feel ill equipped to face is to watch a counselor work through them with your church member.

- Ask the member to e-mail you a short summary of each session. This gives you an opportunity to keep up with the person's progress and get some sense of the counselor's theology and methodology.
- Ask the member to give the counselor permission to talk with you so you can check in with the counselor and get an assessment of how things are going. A helpful counselor will work alongside a pastor, keeping him informed of how the church can wisely love the struggling person. If the counselor is unwilling or won't make time to talk with the pastor, cross him off the referral list.

Professional Counseling

Our criteria for choosing a good church or parachurch counselor apply to professional counseling as well. A licensed professional *Christian* counselor should counsel like a Christian. The term "Christian" can't just be a label; it should characterize the counsel given and the kind of help offered.

We would warn you more strongly against a professional Christian counselor who is weak in his biblical framework of human problems than against a psychologist who does not claim to be Christian. The lines of distinction are at least clear in the latter case. In the former, they are blurry. If a professional Christian counselor offers advice that is largely based on unbiblical therapeutic models, then distinguishing between what stems from the Bible and what stems from an alternate model becomes difficult.

Here's an example. Let's say a professional Christian counselor and a professional secular counselor advise your member to go into his bedroom and punch a pillow when his wife angers him. This seems reasonable. It's certainly better than punching his wife, and the pillow is replaceable. If the professional Christian counselor has advised this, your member might assume that this is biblically based advice. After all, it doesn't seem unloving to others or dishonoring to God to treat a pillow viciously. A professional Christian counselor giving such pillow advice would likely cite Scripture to make his point, maybe showing how Jesus directed his anger appropriately by overturning the money changers' tables and not striking the money changers themselves. And this would seem reasonably biblical to your member. But the problem with this advice is that it's based on a faulty understanding of people: that their negative impulses should be expressed so long as they are directed toward safe objects. This reasoning is only a sad attempt to baptize an unbiblical anthropology. The apostle Paul would scoff at such advice, saying that it merely indulges a "fit of anger," which is a "work of the flesh" (Gal. 5:19–20).

With a psychologist who has no Christian convictions, at least an unbiblical anthropology is in plain view. Counsel from such a source can contain practical insights, but has clear limits. Psychologists may give mental strategies for taking control of obsessive thoughts, uncover patterns of disruptive emotive responses, or provide communicative strategies customized for certain problems, and these can be genuinely helpful. But all of these fall short of life-shaping wisdom. So specialists for certain problems can prove useful to your people, but only when their counsel is submitted to a larger biblical worldview.

For instance, a psychotherapist who specializes in posttraumatic stress disorder will know much about the common experiences of a returning soldier and can recognize warning signs in behavior. But he cannot explain the theological starting point of fear, the reality of danger in a fallen world, or the hope of a re-created one. The same can be true of psychologists who specialize in sleep disorders, Tourette's syndrome, infertility issues, childhood trauma, and more.

Pastor, your job may not be to know as much as the therapist about the observable dynamics of a given condition, but it is to show how your people can respond with faith in God to whatever condition they're in. The wisdom to respond in faith comes only from God's Word. So if your people see secular professional counselors for whatever reason, do not let them think they've replaced the need for biblical guidance from their pastor.

Medical or Psychiatric Help

God created us to comprise body and soul, and these two aspects of our nature interrelate in mysterious and wonderful ways. God declared this design good, but sin corrupted both our bodies and our souls. The fall gave us not only a spiritual bent toward sin, but also a decaying body. Disease corrupts every part of the body, from muscular and cardiovascular systems to endocrine and neurological. We are stewards of the body as much as the soul. Thus, pastors should always encourage regular medical care.

As you care for your members, sometimes more specific medical attention is needed. In the course of counseling, a person may demonstrate evidence of physiologically complicating factors that need medical attention: for example, bizarre or unpredictable behavior, severe emotional swings, or invasive hallucinations.

Is a pastor encouraging spiritual laziness in his member by encouraging him to see a doctor? Only if that person is allowed to think that medications can solve his problems. Meds alone cannot solve the problems of the soul. Medicine is just one tool in the overall biblical approach to care for embodied people, and this tool must never be used in a way that undermines engagement with God through his Word.

A pastor ought to be aware that members who seek medical or psychiatric attention often feel shame for doing so. Such shame can hinder their pursuit of a loving God who understands their weaknesses. You can serve them well by assuring them that they can still trust the Lord and seek to understand the core spiritual issues at play as they are being treated medically. Remind them that they are a mysterious combination of body and soul, and that their bodies (not just their souls) are corrupted by sin. Seeking medical help for the things that go wrong with our bodies is a normal part of living in a fallen world. Though medicine, like any created thing, can be a false refuge from deeper problems, it does not have to function that way. Seeking medical help is not a failure of faith.

How can a pastor help in his member's search for medical or psychiatric help? The answer lies in finding the right kind of doctor. Here is what you need.

A doctor who is competent. Competence involves at least two things: conscientious effort and knowledge of the limits of medicine. Regarding the first, some doctors spend the necessary time and effort to get to know their patients, and others do not. A great way to find out how much attention a person gets with a doctor is to find out how long an appointment is scheduled for. With the pressure of managed care and meeting quotas, some practices will schedule seven or eight patients per hour, which leaves seven to nine minutes for each patient. Such a quick turnaround significantly increases the chance for inattentive diagnosis and monitoring. You want a practice that prioritizes accurately understanding the physiological aspects of the problem before prescribing medicine.

Regarding a doctor's awareness of the limits of medical care, a good psychiatrist knows that his or her focus should be on the medical aspects of the problem and not venture into spiritual, moral, or relational counsel. Medical professionals can offer practical tips for helping physical realities, but life-shaping wisdom and spiritual counsel lie outside their professional territory.

Obviously, a doctor with vibrant faith and competence as a physician can do much good in complementing the spiritual care of the church. If you find a doctor like this, realize what a precious gift it is to you and your church.

A doctor who is willing to communicate with the pastor. Even with the proper releases, some doctors may be uncomfortable speaking with a patient's pastor. You want a doctor who actually welcomes communication with key members of a patient's support system. This indicates that he or she sees the importance of sources of wisdom and support that medicine cannot provide.

A doctor who is affordable. Health insurance is only becoming more complex to figure out. Costs are dependent on whether a doctor is in-network or out. Added to this complexity is the recent reality that many private practices have stopped billing insurance at all because the reimbursement process, red tape, and hassle are so cumbersome that the quality of the practice suffers. Such practices may provide patients with a form that they can send to their insurance company to seek reimbursement on their own. But this does require the patient to float the cost until reimbursement. Your awareness of these realities will enable you to help your member make a wise choice.

CONCLUSION

As a pastor you serve in a role of spiritual authority over your church members' lives (Ezekiel 34; Heb. 13:7; 1 Pet. 5:1–4). But anyone who has pastored knows that his voice is one among many. As you create a referral list, do so carefully. You save yourself a lot of untangling later by helping members choose wisely on the front end and preparing them to listen discerningly to advice.

If the counselor or doctor consistently conflicts with your pastoral counsel, that makes sorting through the mess much more difficult. Struggling people are not helped by conflicting advice. In situations where conflicting advice is causing confusion and pain, it's best to advise a member to look for a new counselor or doctor. This should be done with humility and courtesy to everyone involved.

The bottom line is that you cannot hand off responsibility for the soul of a member to another caregiver, Christian or not. Referral is not a handing off, but a problem-specific supplement to the biblical view of life you are responsible to instill. This process is not always clear, but with the principles laid out, you'll have a good chance of maintaining the biblical discernment you'll need to use outside resources wisely.

A Labor of Love

Good pastors work hard. They do so in the private study and the public pulpit because they believe the Word of God brings life to their people. And they do the same no matter where they are—the front office, the living room, or the neighborhood—because they know God's Word is powerful.

God's Word brings hope to people struggling with problems, but often people need help to see this connection. A pastor and his Bible can do a world of good to a struggling person. That's not a naive or triumphalist thing to say. A pastor can help people know how to respond by faith in Christ to any difficulty, opening them up to receive God's grace for their time of need.

Counseling is a tool—just one of the ministries of the Word among many—to help another person live out wholehearted faith in the gospel of Jesus Christ. You, pastor, are called to use this tool to help bring life to struggling people. Counseling is an opportunity to walk alongside hurting folks, not as a distraction from your ministry, but rather as a necessary and good part of your labor on behalf of the church.

As you counsel, we want you to be confident that Scripture

has everything you need to address a person pastorally, no matter how complex the problem. You won't be able to solve every aspect of every person's trouble, but you will be able to show people how to walk by faith in Christ.

Our task has been to remind you of the great and noble task of shepherding God's flock. It's a hard labor, but a worthy labor. It's a labor that Christ has called you to do, following his example as our Great Shepherd. The shepherd loves his sheep and gives up his life for them. What about you, pastor? Are you willing to do the same?

A Quick Checklist for the Counseling Process

This checklist is intended to help you prepare for individual counseling cases. Remember, you are seeking to address the present problem, display the relevance of the gospel, and help people grow in Christlikeness. You do this by following a *method* for exploring the heart, which works itself out in the counseling *process*. Both are outlined below.

THE METHOD

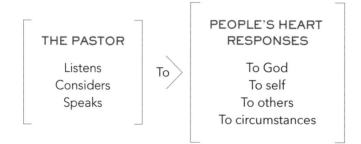

THE PASTOR

Listens
Considers
Speaks

To

PEOPLE'S HEART RESPONSES

To God
To self
To others
To circumstances

THE PROCESS

The counseling process is simply the framework for exploring the heart through the above method.

Before the Initial Meeting

- ☐ Send and receive a personal background form, or informally ask for a summary of the problem.
- ☐ Mobilize resources—books or people—in preparation for the first meeting.
- ☐ Prepare questions and talking points according to the list below for the initial meeting.

The Initial Meeting(s)

- ☐ Establish a relational connection.
- ☐ Explore the concern (use the methodology above).
- ☐ Display hope.
- ☐ Set expectations.
- ☐ Assign prep work.

The Ongoing Meetings

- ☐ Get an update.
- ☐ Ask about prep work.
- ☐ Continue to explore the concerns.
- ☐ Offer redemptive remedies.

The Final Meeting(s)

- ☐ Review the main themes of counseling.
- ☐ Plan for regular care.

What Is Christian Counseling?

If you have ever looked online or shopped for a counselor, you've noticed a dizzying array of counseling models available on today's evangelical market—Emotion Focused Therapy (EFT), Cognitive Behavior Therapy (CBT), Dialectic Behavior Therapy (DBT), to name just a few. To date, there are dozens of models that Christians use to counsel.

This section is intentionally brief. We want to give a definition of counseling that may help you determine the direction you should take your church's counseling ministry or perhaps discern the counseling philosophy of a local professional.

In our view, counseling that is Christian, or biblical in its most basic form, is a ministry of the Word by which Christians help others understand how their hearts are actively responding to God amid their specific life circumstances, and how faith in Christ Jesus changes those responses.

To unpack this a bit, we could say that a Christian counselor addresses a person's thoughts, beliefs, desires, feelings, decisions, and actions in light of God's revealed will for how people ought to function. As people relate rightly to Christ through faith in his gospel, their hearts are progressively transformed to relate rightly to everything else—to others, to self, and to circumstances. Being right with God restores right relations to everything else.

Counseling requires skill and wisdom to parse out the complex issues in life. Yet Christian counseling is unapologetically guided by a biblical view of God and his intentions toward people. It unapologetically understands Christ as the means and goal of change. While acknowledging human trouble as complex in its dynamic expression, it unapologetically uses old biblical categories like pride, lust, anger, fear, hatred, revenge, foolishness, ignorance, confusion, and suffering. The contours of counseling follow the narrative contours of an ancient book of divine wisdom, a book that cannot be domesticated and is always relevant to the farthest depths of the human experience.

Personal Background Form

[Name of Your Church]

[A digital version of this form is available for free at http:// crossway.org/PCappendix. The form was developed in part from the Personal Data Inventory in Jay E. Adams, *Competent to Counsel: Introduction to Nouthetic Counseling* (Grand Rapids: Zondervan, 1970), as well as unpublished training material from Stuart Scott.]

This inventory gives us an overview of your story so we can understand how best to serve you. Please fill it out honestly and thoughtfully. We will handle the information with loving prudence.

GENERAL INFORMATION

We'll need your basic information to contact you and get a general sense of what occupies your life.

Name _____ Date of birth _____

Address _____

Zip code _____

Age _____ Sex _____ Referred by _____

Marital status: ☐ Single ☐ Engaged ☐ Married
☐ Separated ☐ Divorced ☐ Widowed

Home phone _____ Work phone _____

Employer _____

Position _____

Time with current employer _____

Education (degree level) _____

Give ten words that describe your personality.

_____

_____

_____

_____

MARRIAGE AND FAMILY

Few relationships are as involved in your daily experience as family. We'll need the basics to understand how best to help you. If there is anything you think we should know that isn't mentioned in this section, please feel free to write it in.

If single, please describe your attitude toward your singleness.

_____

_____

_____

If married, please fill out the following:

Spouse _____

Date of birth _____ Age _____

Occupation _____   How long employed _____

Home phone _____   Work phone _____

Date of marriage _____   Length of dating _____

Give a brief statement of circumstances of meeting and dating.

_____

_____

_____

Has either of you been previously married? _____

To whom? _____

Have you ever been separated from one another? _____

Have you ever filed for divorce? _____

Children:

Name	Age	Sex	Education	Living?	Stepchild?
_____	___	___	_____	_____	_____
_____	___	___	_____	_____	_____
_____	___	___	_____	_____	_____

GROWING UP YEARS

While we don't think that childhood experiences strictly determine how we respond as adults, we do recognize that past experience influences present perspectives. So we will ask you to describe the family you came from. Again, if there is anything you think we should know that isn't mentioned in this section, please feel free to write it in.

Describe your relationship to your father.

_____

_____

_____

_____

_____

Describe your relationship to your mother.

_____

_____

_____

_____

_____

Did you live with anyone other than your parents? If so, please describe the relationship.

_____

_____

_____

_____

Describe relationships with siblings (include number and birth order).

_____

_____

_____

_____

Describe any significant events in your family life growing up.

_____

_____

_____

_____

_____

HEALTH

We are physical as well as spiritual beings, and our bodies are important factors in our experience. Though we counselors are not medical professionals, it's helpful for us to know general facts about your health.

Describe your health generally.

_____

Do you have any chronic condition or significant illness, injury, or disability?

_____

Professional Medical Help

Physician's name and address:

_____

_____

Date of last medical exam _____

Report _____

Have you ever seen a psychiatrist or psychologist? _____

If yes, please explain.

_____

_____

Psychiatrist's/psychologist's name and address:

_____

_____

Date of last appointment _____

Report _____

Are you willing to sign a release of information form so that your counselor may attain social, psychiatric, or other medical records?

_____

Current medication(s)	Dosage
_____	_____
_____	_____
_____	_____
_____	_____

Have you ever used drugs for anything other than medical purposes? _____ If yes, please explain.

_____

_____

_____

Substance Use	Yes/No	How frequently and how much?
Alcoholic beverages?	_____	_____
Caffeine?	_____	_____
Tobacco products?	_____	_____

OTHER

Have you ever been arrested? _____ If yes, please explain.

_____

_____

Have you ever had interpersonal problems on the job? _____
If yes, please explain.

_____

_____

Have you ever had a severe emotional upset? _____
If yes, please explain.

_____

_____

Women Only

Please explain any menstrual symptoms that affect your functioning, such as tension or a tendency to cry.

_____

_____

_____

If you are married, is your husband supportive of your coming for counseling? Is he willing to be involved?

_____

_____

Do you feel safe at home?

_____

_____

Children Only
How open are you with your parents/caretakers about your troubles?

_____

_____

Do you feel safe at home?

_____

_____

Spiritual Pursuit
While we view all of human life as spiritual in nature, our religious identification indicates a lot about how we exercise our spirituality. We ask this information to get a better grasp of how you pursue God in your life experience.

Church you attend _____

Are you a member? _____

What year did you start attending the church? _____

What year did you join the church? _____

Aside from attending, what roles or responsibilities do you have at the church?

_____

_____

What denominations or religions have you been involved with in the past? Please note any significant changes in your religious life.

_____

_____

Which statement best describes your relationship to Jesus Christ? If you don't like any of these, write your own.

- ☐ I follow Jesus Christ as my Lord and Savior.
- ☐ I am interested in Jesus Christ and am still learning what it means to follow him.
- ☐ I used to follow Jesus Christ, but no longer do.
- ☐ I am not interested in following Jesus Christ as my Lord and Savior.

If you pray, describe your prayer life.

_____

_____

_____

How often do you read the Bible?

☐ Never   ☐ Occasionally   ☐ Often   ☐ Daily

Does God have anything to do with the problem that troubles you? Explain.

_____

_____

_____

Problem Checklist
We realize that problems can't be described fully in a form like this. This is our attempt to get only the lay of the land so that we can more efficiently explore what we need to in order to help. If your problem is not listed here, feel free to write it in.

☐ Alcohol overuse ☐ Depression ☐ Motivation / apathy

☐ Anger / aggression ☐ Desire, overwhelming ☐ Obsessions, compulsions

☐ Anxiety ☐ Drug use ☐ Pain, chronic physical

☐ Attention / concentration ☐ Eating problems ☐ Parenting issues

☐ Bitterness ☐ Fatigue / tiredness ☐ Relational difficulty

☐ Change in lifestyle ☐ Fear ☐ Same-sex attraction

☐ Childhood issues ☐ Financial problems ☐ Sexual dysfunction

☐ Communication ☐ Guilt ☐ Sexual lust / immorality

☐ Conflict, interpersonal ☐ Insecurity ☐ Sleeplessness

☐ Confusion ☐ Loneliness ☐ Thoughts, invasive

☐ Decision making ☐ Moodiness ☐ Other _____

Problem Overview in Your Own Words

Describe what problem brings you here.

_____

_____

What have you done about the problem so far?

_____

_____

What are your expectations for counseling?

_____

_____

Is there any other information that we should know?

_____

_____

A Simple Method for Taking Notes and Organizing Data

Although many situations will require you to step into a counseling situation without preparation or a chance to take notes, note taking is certainly the ideal regular practice. Taking notes in counseling is important for many reasons. It cuts down on confusion between multiple persons you are helping. It aids in retention of important details. It helps you reflect on and pray for the one you are helping. It records important statements for analysis. And it helps you distinguish more important issues from less important ones.

Remember that anything written during a counseling situation can be subpoenaed in a court of law, so it is best to keep the information factual and not speculative. For example, writing "Reports suicidal thinking in the past, but assures no desire to harm self presently" is better than writing "This person has thought about suicide in the past and could possibly kill himself."

SETUP

Proper organization will help you immensely when you review the session for prayer and reflection. As you get your own system down, the notes become "invisible" in the sense that the process of discerning what you wrote down and trying to recover your initial thoughts will become shorter and less laborious. Here are a few practical tips:

- Each counseling case should have its own manila folder, which should be kept in a private and secure place.
- Notes should be free but organized. A suggested page setup is below. Please remember that this is only a suggestion. Each counselor should develop his or her own system.
- You prepare the top margin and the left margin prior to a counseling session. The top margin is for logistical information, and the left margin is for themes you want to explore or biblical insights you want to share.
- A session will often go in unexpected directions, so you don't want to keep to your plan too strictly. On the other hand, it can be a helpful guide if the conversation drifts too far off course.

Top Margin

Place vital logistical information on the top line: name, session number, and date.

Left Margin

Place prepared themes to explore or questions to ask in the left margin. Keep in mind that for any theme, you can explore how the counselee's heart is responding to God, to others, to self, or to circumstance.

John & Susie Everyman   Session 1   5/18/2016

Update

1. Relational Conflict:
Describe how you respond to the other.
What do you want from the other?
How long has this conflict been going on?
Do you have similar conflict with others?

2. Fear at Work (John):
Describe your anxiety at work.
What is your worst fear in life?
How does this relate to your conflict at home?

3. Bitterness (Susie):
When did it start?
What caused it?
What would make it go away?

Scripture Meditation

Psalm 27
vv. 1–3, experience of fear
vv. 4–8, seeking refuge
vv. 9–10, safety in relationship with God
vv. 11–14, faith response: patience, confidence, trust

(J) *Been a tough week*
   "Stress at work always makes it worse at home."

   (S) *conflict for 3 years, ever since taking new job*
(J) *"Susie can't understand me anymore. Doesn't try."*
        No real conflict with anyone else.

   (J) *Worst fear is losing job, ending up on street.*
     "She doesn't know what it's like, the pressure of
                making it in the world."

        [*Fear of Failure?*]
   (S) *John says that all the time. Gets mad when I*
ask *about his day.*
        "He can't take criticism at all."

   (J) *"Susie is a very critical person."*
      – *about who I am*
      – *about finances*
      – *about my weight*

        [*S manipulative response to J ?*]

      (S) *"I have to admit I'm bitter."*
          – *doesn't care for me*
   – *obsessed with himself and his own problems*

You may also enter brief outlines of biblical exploration/ instruction. Open the Bible and ask questions of the counselee to draw out observations on the text.

You may write down any prep work you will assign here.

Main Section

The main section is where you take notes during the session. You don't have to write notes in a linear fashion, but rather can clump ideas together as you go. Here is a helpful code for keeping things straight while writing quickly:

(J) and (S)   To distinguish between speakers in couples counseling, it will be helpful to write the person's initial and circle it next to the information each one gives.

" "   Use quotation marks for salient quotes. Everything else can be written as summaries of what the counselees say.

[ ]   Bracket comments that are your private thoughts during the session. You'll often get hunches you'll want to get down on paper so you won't forget. Brackets assure you'll know these are your own thoughts and not the words of your counselees.

Processing Your Notes

After the session is over and you are returning to your notes, your primary task is to seek the Lord for wisdom in prayer and consideration of Scripture. You are asking for insight into both the suffering and the sin you are observing—in sum, ask what is hindering individuals from responding to others, themselves, and their circumstances with a heart of love and faith in the living God.

As you do this, consider the notes before you, seeking to recognize themes in the information you've written. A good way to do this is the circle-and-number method.

1. Circle statements or facts that seem most important.
2. Consider whether they fall into common themes. You don't even have to label the themes at this point, but can just put a number on each of them.

3. Place the same number for all of the circled items that are similar.

4. Write out a list of themes at the bottom of the page once you have them all identified.

5. Prayerfully consider what biblical principles address the themes you see emerge from your session. Always link biblical insight to the gospel of Jesus Christ, but also think as broadly as possible of the available biblical material.

6. Transfer those themes to the left margin of a new sheet of notes prepared for the next session.

Special Thanks

Thankfulness should be like breathing to us. God is the source of everything good, and we happily acknowledge his grace to us. This grace finds its highest expression in the person and work of Jesus Christ, who loved us and gave himself up for us. Even an entire life dedicated to thanking him is dismally poor in comparison to so rich a gift.

We are grateful to 9Marks for providing the perfect platform to share our burden to help fellow pastors care well for their people. Thank you to our dear friends Ryan, Jonathan, Mark, and Bobby. We are grateful to our friends at Crossway for the same reasons.

We're both blessed to serve wonderful churches, Clifton Baptist and Capitol Hill Baptist. We each labor beside an excellent team of godly men and count it one of the greatest privileges of life to do so. We are also grateful for The Southern Baptist Theological Seminary and its commitment to the local church.

Of the people who deserve thanks, our two Sarahs get the greatest portion. Mrs. Pierre and Mrs. Reju, without you, our lives would be cinematic tragedies. But with you, they are happy tales.

General Index

Scripture Index

9Marks

Building Healthy Churches

9Marks exists to equip church leaders with a biblical vision and practical resources for displaying God's glory to the nations through healthy churches.

To that end, we want to see churches characterized by these nine marks of health:

1 Expositional Preaching
2 Biblical Theology
3 A Biblical Understanding of the Gospel
4 A Biblical Understanding of Conversion
5 A Biblical Understanding of Evangelism
6 Biblical Church Membership
7 Biblical Church Discipline
8 Biblical Discipleship
9 Biblical Church Leadership

Find all our Crossway titles
and other resources at
www.9Marks.org